Thank you for sharing your stories . . . keep up the fight!
~ Office of Senator Elizabeth Warren

I enjoyed this book as a fellow attorney CT attorney. Her writing style keeps the reader entertained while describing an area of the law that many people wish to avoid dealing with. Debt is a fact of life for most Americans and best to know how to resolve financial problems when they do arise. Kudos to the author to writing this informative book.
~ Chris McCormick, bankruptcy attorney

Really pleasantly surprised, a book about debt, collections and foreclosure that's fun to read. Some nice nuggets ~ Cinco de Mayo resulted from one of the largest repo actions in history ~ between courtroom and case reminiscences and how to deal with excessive credit card debt. Pragmatic and empathetic at once, no easy feat.
~ RR Hicks, author of *The Ceremony of Innocence* & *The Falcon*

I teach personal finance classes, where questions about debt and foreclosure issues always come in volume . . . The author makes the responsible choice not to give much specific advice . . .That really sets it apart from the ocean of books out there that sell hyperbole . . .the author recognizes what an emotional process it can all be, and takes care to address the scare tactics that debt collectors sometimes employ
~Sharif Erik-Soussi, Capital Community College

got debt?

Dispatches
from the front lines of
America's financial crisis

Sarah Poriss

For more information on the author, please go to:

SarahPoriss.com

All clients and judges mentioned in this work are fictionalized and composites of several individuals and many issues over many years; nothing herein should be construed as legal advice

FORLORN HOPE PUBLISHING

Forlorn Hope Publishing
Forlornhopepub.com

For my father

Everybody knows the dice are loaded,
Everybody rolls with their fingers crossed.
~ Leonard Cohen

Preface to the Second Edition

I published the first edition of *Got Debt, Dispatches From the Front Lines of America's Debt Crisis* in October, 2017. At the time the economy wasn't treading water, wasn't booming. It was just, or so it seemed to me, moving along in a hopeful direction while I was still cleaning up the detritus left from the Recession.

The economy eventually did take off – at least according to the media in all its forms. Unemployment dropped like a rock, the stock market soared, economic indicators indicated "great things," everybody was working, houses were selling – although nowhere near the rate of the early 2000s, but we all know how that worked out so lower growth there was just fine.

Through all this good news I noticed a few things. For one, I was as busy as ever with foreclosure and debt cases and they weren't leftovers from 2008, they were new. The economy may have been zipping along but homes were still going into foreclosure, credit cards were being maxed out, late payments piled up as before, banks were issuing default notices, and collection firms, lean and mean after consolidation and some house-cleaning during the Recession, were enjoying a golden age.

It doesn't take a rocket scientist or a lawyer who deals in consumer debt every day to realize that wages – the regular working wage of the regular middle-class worker – hadn't changed at all. At least not in comparison with inflation.

The dollar is not going as far as it did and that's a trend that doesn't look like it's going to change anytime soon, despite constant promises from politicians.

People continue to supplement lagging incomes with credit. Still. They're just doing it today a little more quietly than during and immediately after the Recession. Debt back then was front page news, now it's stuck – when it's mentioned at all – back in the "Consumer Help Team" section.

Debt is still there, the crisis is still there, the coverage is not and as the coverage goes, so goes the awareness.

Not too long ago, I read a review of a terrific movie, *Hell or High Water*, a movie very much about foreclosure. It was shot on location in West Texas and Eastern New Mexico. The cinematography is brilliant – as noted in the review.

The reviewer loved the movie, loved the performances, loved everything but had this criticism (I'm paraphrasing): *"They really overdid it with the boarded up buildings, empty houses with foreclosure signs, billboards for pawn shops and companies that buy distressed homes."*

I've been to conferences in Texas – Florida as well – and I can personally attest that the filmmakers didn't overdo anything, they simply shot what was there on the side of roads not interstates.

The review simply wants us to believe what is not supported by fact – the Recession is over and that foreclosures and crushing debt are fading away with it.

Debt is still everywhere and it affects almost everyone in one way or another. Pretending it's not is not only irresponsible, it is setting the stage for another recession and new generations afflicted to be by it. I share here the story of the law firm that used to foreclose on medical debt, and when that became public and the firm fired by the hospital after the shameful news broke, how it moved on to focus on collection of old credit card debt- a more "under the radar" type of work as there is less general sympathy for the person who couldn't pay a credit card than someone who couldn't pay a medical bill. So has gone the story of crushing debt—we have become desensitized to it, and so overwhelmed by our own situations we have no empathy left for others. It has become old news, it's that simple.

Hence this new edition.

Sarah Poriss
West Hartford, Conn.
March, 2019

Sarah Poriss

Forward

There's a scene in the movie *An Officer and a Gentleman* where Mayo (Richard Gere) is in big trouble, and Sergeant Foley (Louis Gossett, Jr.) makes him stay on base for the weekend and puts him through the calisthenics session from hell. In pouring rain. For hours on end. Mayo looks like he's going to break and Foley pours it on, screaming at him to "DNR" – quit. Mayo won't. Foley presses, finally Mayo sobs, "I got nowhere else to go."

That was me. Well not exactly - but I was at a point in my life where I had nowhere else to go. I had been working for 2 1/2 years for a blind attorney. She was an Assistant Attorney General for the State of Connecticut and I was hired as her reader and driver. Essentially, I was her reasonable accommodation under the Americans With Disability Act.

The job's requirements were not exactly stringent, a driver's license and the ability to read. I wasn't doing anything better at the time so, I thought why not, I had the license and I read. A lot. I applied. I'm told I beat out fifty other drivers who could also read.

Despite the inauspicious application process, the job was my first experience with the legal world. It was … interesting.

Fast forward a couple of years and I had grown out of it. I had learned enough about the legal system that I knew I could be a legal secretary or paralegal and make much more money than I did as an assistant. I started looking around, but no one would hire me. I thought I interviewed well, I knew I was qualified, I was interested in working in a law firm or other legal setting, but no offers. I felt a little like Dustin Hoffman in *Tootsie* before he had to resort to dressing as a woman.

I tried to apply for a paralegal position at the Attorney General's office, but they did not want to hire me away from the attorney I was working for. It did not matter that I was already trained for the job openings and was qualified, if not more qualified, than most of the candidates for those positions. I just wasn't getting anywhere applying.

Out of pride I quit the assistant job, frustrated that others less qualified were hired for the better paying and more career-track jobs. I took some temp jobs, then I had a conversation about my future with a girlfriend who happened to be in law school at the time. I told her I thought my options came down to teaching, a degree in social work, or applying to law school. After all, I thought, I had nowhere else to go! No one would hire me to be their legal secretary or paralegal!

She thought for less than a second, then said, "Go to law school."

I thought about it for a minute, said "My father would love that."

She replied, "Well, do you love your father?"

"Of course."

"Then make him happy and apply."

A day or so later, she dropped off her study books for the LSAT test. I signed up, studied, took it (a long day), applied to a couple of local law schools, and was accepted to the University of Connecticut. Just like that.

How messed up is it that I could not get hired as a secretary or paralegal but I was going to be allowed to be a lawyer? What does that say about the profession?

Think about it this way, what if you can't get a hospital to hire you as an orderly, but you can get into medical school?

At the University of Connecticut School of Law, my classmates and I talked about our reasons for going to law school. One friend was honest enough to say he didn't care what he did, he was going for the highest paying job (he has since taken a job doing what the blind attorney did and works for the state representing our Department of Children and Families).

I said, "I want to save the world." I did admit, though, that after three years of graduate school (at which point I would be in my early thirties with a lot of student loan debt) that I would probably accept the job that paid me the most as well.

By the third year of law school you usually know where you are going to work after graduation. At least that's how it worked when I began practicing, several years before the economy crashed in 2008. But I reached my third year without lining up anything.

Late Fall, my last year, I saw a notice for an opening at a small firm called Consumer Law Group. I researched the firm, found it worked on consumer protection issues. It seemed to me like a legal aid job, but with a decent paycheck.

I interviewed, talked the talk, and was hired. After about a year there I gravitated toward working on debt and credit issues-- debt collection harassment, identity theft, errors on credit reports, that kind of work.

It didn't take long for me to realize there were very few lawyers, if any, who regularly defended people being sued for unpaid credit card debt. I found a niche and I went solo.

Soon after that I was referred some homeowners in foreclosure and found that not only did I enjoy representing people in debt, I was good at it. It looked like foreclosures would be a smaller, but still significant, part of my young practice.

Then the recession hit in 2008 and foreclosures were rampant. Unfortunately, Connecticut had (and still has) one of the highest rates of foreclosure in the country. Those early cases allowed me to begin playing an important role in defending homeowners in foreclosure.

This book consists of everything I have written since my first years as a solo attorney. It is an attempt to better understand my clients. It is a study of the average person's response to being in debt and the effects being in debt has on the typical, hard-working person. It is an examination of what I have had to do to juggle helping people in financial distress with making a living myself.

There are a few keys to working with people in debt, not the least of which is getting past the assumption that if they are in debt they have no money.

Another obstacle is helping them get over – or at least deal with – the shame, embarrassment, anger and frustration that is endemic in the working middle-class. They earn too much to qualify for legal aid assistance, but don't think they earn enough to afford an attorney.

This book is an attempt to humanize the causes of debt, to de-stigmatize the phenomenon of overwhelming debt. It is an effort to get us all talking about debt, money, credit and credit scores so that we don't have to feel so alone in the struggle, so that we can turn fear and shame into knowledge and empowerment.

Start talking about debt, now. With your family, friends, neighbors, co-workers and especially your kids. I hope this book helps get that conversation started.

Sarah Poriss
Hartford, Conn.
Summer, 2017

Sarah Poriss

x

1. Going Solo

I used to work out of a spare bedroom in our 1916 craftsman-style bungalow. When I left my job as an associate at the consumer protection firm, I didn't expect to start a solo practice. I was burned out and took some hourly contract work helping a firm review discovery documents. This allowed me to work from home.

I was given a little training on each case I worked on, then I would log into a database from my laptop, often from bed or the living room couch, and scroll through thousands of pages of documents on the screen looking for incriminating statements made by executives of companies charged with insider trading violations. The money was great, I could listen to the radio or have the TV on in the background, and no one bothered me.

But within about a week of leaving the firm, my old boss, with whom I kept a good relationship, called and said there were people calling asking for me but with issues he couldn't help with. My old firm specialized in plaintiff-side consumer class actions and individual cases against companies that committed consumer scams and other unfair acts and practices. We were the good guys representing the little guy.

When I worked there I was assigned to handle debt collection harassment claims. These were straightforward and interesting. I was constantly amazed at the creative ways the debt collectors got around the prohibitions of the law that regulated them. The law included a provision that if my client won, we could collect our attorney's fees from the debt collector. My firm took these cases on a contingent basis which allowed the low-income client to be represented without having to pay a retainer up front.

I was also assigned to help senior citizens referred to the office by the AARP or local legal services organizations for pro bono help when they were sued on an unpaid credit card balance. As a practice, we did not take on the defense of these matters, mostly because there was no way we could get paid-- there is no attorney's fee provision in breach of contract matters, which is the claim against you when you do not pay your credit cards. I would walk these seniors through how to respond to the suit and tell them what to do when the case was scheduled for a hearing or a pre-trial.

The people whom I had helped before leaving the firm eventually received a trial. They called the firm back for more help and found out I'd left. My old boss called me asking if I wanted him to send them my way. I agreed, not knowing where it would lead.

The first person to call me was a woman supporting her grandchildren who was being sued by her credit card company for a couple thousand bucks. I remember she had a gold front tooth and a fancy manicure. When we spoke, I said it was nice to hear from her and I could help her but that I'd have to charge her. She said "OK," and I signed up my first client.

With my old boss sending people like this my way, I had 20 clients in a month. I worked out of that spare bedroom for two and a half years. I had no overhead and could pocket almost all the fees I earned. I didn't mind having to meet with clients in public places, and I don't believe they minded either. After all, I was pretty much the only lawyer around who represented people in debt in court for a reasonable price.

Within a few weeks, I had scoped out some good meeting places and would set appointments according to where the client lived or worked. If they were from East of the Connecticut River, I would suggest the Burger King on Silver Lane in East Hartford. It was about a 10-minute drive from my house and everyone seemed to know where it was.

If they were from West Hartford, I would suggest the Dunkin Donuts on the corner of New Britain Avenue and South Main Street. This one was a combo Dunkin and Baskin Robbins ice cream shop, and for some reason there was a separate room inside the shop that had a few tables and you could close the door. If you were lucky and the stay-at-home-mom coffee club or AA meeting hadn't settled into that room, it was a great place to meet.

One time a client who lived in Hartford's South end needed to meet that day. Problem was my car was in the shop. I asked if he could meet me at the McDonald's on Prospect Avenue since I could walk to the meeting. He and I ended up meeting there several times over the next year.

I wasn't worried about having these sensitive conversations in public. I found no one really bothered to listen to our discussions and the client really couldn't afford to be picky. Neither could I.

Occasionally, after I got to know a client, I wouldn't mind if we met at my house. I would even encourage this in the summer, and we'd meet on my big front porch, which I nicknamed my "outdoor office". It had some nice comfortable chairs and a big coffee table, so if I needed to review some documents or if the client needed to sign something, there was plenty of space.

Then there was a shift in my universe and multiple forces led me to get my first office. The guy who took over for me when I left my position at the firm was looking to go out on his own and to share office space with someone, and my father had died leaving a house full of furniture, some of which was perfect to furnish an office. If you looked close, my old conference room table was a Formica-topped pedestal kitchen table.

I still believe I would be happy working out of a home office. There are definitely pros to separating your work space from your personal space. My husband was starting to resent the fact that I'd turn on my computer and start checking emails before even getting in the shower or taking the dog out in the morning. But I don't miss the feeling that if I'm home, I could be working.

The best thing about getting an office was the increased productivity. When I had an appointment to meet a client at one of my "satellite" offices, a one-hour appointment would turn into a two-hour commitment with the travel to and from the location. I, of course, always wanted to arrive first so I would arrive early and wait. Luckily, since I was good at confirming the appointments with clients in advance, I was only stood up once. And I got a call the next day from the client who didn't show to let me know she had gotten in a car accident. I sure as heck got all those details and referred her to a colleague who handles personal injury and accident matters. But with an office, I could work right up to the minute the client walked in the door, and if they were late or no-showed, I could just keep on billing hours on another client's file.

My space was previously occupied by a local non-profit organization called the Brazilian Alliance. They used to occupy almost the entire half of the floor of the building, but were forced to downsize when the economy turned sour and their sources of funding started to dry up.

I took over a 500-square foot section that was divided into one large room and one small room. I set up the small room as the conference room, and had the management company put up half-walls in the large room to delineate a reception area and two work cubicles.

A couple of months after I moved in, another business moved into the rest of the space vacated by the Brazilian Alliance. I met the owner when the management company brought him to see my space when they couldn't get into the office he was looking to rent to show how big the office was and the ceiling height.

Henry was the biggest black man I had ever met. Add a long set

5

of dreadlocks and he was quite the imposing figure. I figured he'd be a great guy to walk me to my car if we worked past dark. As tough as he looked, he opened his mouth into the nicest, whitest smile I'd ever seen, as if he was a model for an orthodontist's office. He turned out to be one of the sweetest people I've ever met in business and he turned into one of my biggest fans. When I come over to talk and he had someone in his office, he referred to me as his attorney or "mi abogada," since he was actually Puerto Rican. I felt honored.

"What kind of business do you have, Henry?" I asked him when he moved in.

"I lend money. Small amounts, up to $1000."

Oh great, I thought, a loan shark. My business was helping people out of debt, he was working to get people into debt.

"I'd love to talk to you more about that someday," I said, "And I hope none of your customers come to me for help."

"Actually, a lot of people come to me because their credit is screwed up and they can't get money anywhere else," he explained.

Hand in hand with my helping people get out of debt is working on fixing up their credit. Maybe this would be a good working relationship after all.

Although I have never sent anyone his way, he had me come over to his office several times to review papers his clients had received and I have gotten a couple of new clients from him. You never know, I guess.

The other great thing about Henry being next door was that he was heavy into security. One day I was chatting with him in the hallway, we were crossing paths coming out of the restrooms, and he asked me if I knew how to buy a foreclosed property. I said, "Sure, it's easy, the listings are posted online now."

"Yeah," he said, "but those services are really expensive."

"No, the court lists foreclosure sales on their website now and it's free."

While I tried to prevent my homeowner clients' houses from going on the auction block, they were legitimate sales and if Henry wanted to buy a house for an investment, no reason I shouldn't show him how to get all the info he needed.

I went into his office and stepped behind his desk to show him how to get to the court website to find upcoming foreclosure sales and all the details you need about the properties.

As I was standing over his shoulder, I noticed he had a small set of speakers connected to his laptop. That explained the R&B music I'd hear through the heating vents most afternoons. Tucked between the left speaker and the wall was a big wad of cash. I mean BIG. You couldn't see it if you were sitting anywhere but in Henry's desk chair.

A couple of weeks later, Henry asked me if I noticed his cameras in the hallway. "Cameras?" I asked. And he took me into his office where he had a new monitor set up on his desk, and you could see two images of the hallway outside his office door. I went back into the hallway and saw them mounted to the support beam 10 feet up- one pointed to his door; the other was pointing down the hallway toward the elevator, so he could see who was coming and who was standing at his door.

"Very cool," I said, and thought, if you're going to have that kind of cash on you at any given time, cameras were an excellent idea. He said he had two more cameras but hadn't decided where to connect them yet. He offered to have one mounted outside my office door, which was around the corner at the end of the hallway, so that I could get my own monitor. I didn't take him up on it, it seemed like he had security taken care of for the entire floor.

New office, lots of worries, but it was good to know that security was not one of them.

§

Recently, I was sort of interviewed about what I do. My neighbors asked me to pick up their 12-year-old son from school, he was getting home late from a field trip to Boston, they were tied up at work and in meetings, and I was available to help.

He got in my car, we talked about how his trip to the museum was, then he fell silent. He's a great kid, I've known him since he was about two years old, he's very smart, musical and athletic and he's the quiet sensitive type so I did not expect a lot of conversation.

As we drove down Washington Street, I pointed out the courthouse that I go to all the time.

He said, "Oh yeah you're a lawyer. Do you ever have scary cases?"

"Do you mean do I do criminal law?" I asked back.

"Yeah."

"Nope, I help people with mortgage foreclosures."

"What does that mean?"

I paused for a second, then explained that when people want to buy a house they borrow money to buy the house. And when they can't make the payments, they are taken to court for not making their payments. And, if they can't make their payments, they have to move out of their houses.

Finished with the Cliff Notes version, I added, "So, I guess it can be pretty scary."

He took that in for a moment or two, then, asked "Why don't you do criminal law?"

"It just isn't something I ever was interested in or ever had experience with," I answered, "I think it's scary enough when a client of mine has to move out of their house, I would be terrified if because of me someone had to go to jail."

He nodded, "So are you good at Monopoly?"

"I don't know what you mean!"

"You know with all the buying and selling of houses and mortgages."

Of course! It caught me off guard, I said something about I hadn't played in a long time, we'd have to play and see how good I am at it.

I love how he made the connection between what I do and the game of Monopoly.

9

But he didn't stop there, "Do your clients tell the truth?"

I said, "Yes, sometimes my clients are put under oath and should tell the truth . . . but, even when people are put under oath sometimes they don't tell the truth. Sometimes."

That seemed to surprise him a bit and I immediately felt a little bad, like maybe I was being too cynical with a 12-year-old. But it didn't seem to faze him and he moved on to, "Are you friends with your clients?"

"Not really, it's not recommended that lawyers become friends with her clients . . . though I have worked with some people for so long they're almost like family.

"You know, you get along with them, you have to deal with them once in a while, but you don't tell them what you would tell your friends."

He nodded acceptance, moved on to, "Since you have to go in court and speak in front of people, do you like public speaking?"

"Sure," was my immediate reply, then I thought for a second, and added, "but if you told me when I was younger I would be doing as much public speaking as I do, I probably never would've left my bedroom."

"Do you have to convince the judge to help your clients, like you see lawyers arguing in court on TV?"

"Yeah, the judge comes out in a black robe, everyone has to stand up and it's very official. Sometimes I have to tell my clients' story to get the judge to give my clients what they're looking for."

10

He thought about that for a second, pulled out a folder full of homework, asked, "Are your clients afraid?"

"When they first call me, they are usually afraid of something, like they think they have to move out of their house in a very short period of time. But I explain that I can usually get them more time, maybe save the house, at least get them the opportunity to figure out what they're going to do or where they're going to live next."

He made some kind of sound of agreement and dove into his homework, while I just drove and marveled.

I think everyone should have to talk to a 12-year-old once in a while and explain what they do. It gives you a different perspective on how you spend your time every day.

Conversations like this would make everybody a better person.

§

I had a professor in law school who proclaimed loud and clear at least once a week that "Your goal as lawyers should be to *never* be in a casebook." He would usually say it while brandishing a big heavy casebook.

He wasn't referring to world shattering decisions like *Brown v. Board of Education*, he meant the contract cases that could have been settled amicably, tort cases where even a modicum of common sense would have kept them in the lower courts, property cases that mindlessly escalated . . .

. . . Cases that took years and years, appeal after appeal before some judge, somewhere, finally addressed the issue, ended the thing and established new or upheld old law.

Long, drawn out cases belong in case books, Dickens novels, and Larry Ellison's biography.

So when a new client facing foreclosure comes to me armed to the teeth with printouts of California and Massachusetts cases where appellate and/or supreme courts have ruled for homeowners and against banks I cringe, sigh, and go into one of the major parts of my job: managing expectations.

First, foremost, I point out how many years the cases took, how costly they were. Then, how very much, despite the insistence of a chunk of the internet, those cases are outliers. Halley's Comet or total eclipse rarities.

My goal – my absolute, unshakable goal-- is to get the best outcome possible, as early as possible, to relieve the stress my clients are under. This does not include attacking the banks – I'll leave that to Elizabeth Warren, Matt Tiabbi et al. – and it most certainly does not include getting the client 'a free house.'

All the better to stay out of the casebooks . . . and get the job done.

§

One of the most accurate portrayals of what it's like to run a small law firm in this century is *Better Call Saul.* This has nothing to do with working with someone like Mike, or filming 2am attorney ads surreptitiously on Air Force bases, or any one of main character, Jimmy McGill's, dozen other antics.

It's not any of his personal quirks: the flashes of legal genius, his skill as a flim-flam man, his deft touch with the elderly client.

The authenticity of Jimmy is his need for clients and that which comes with them and allows lawyers to continue to be lawyers – money. Jimmy needs every retainer he can lay his hands on. Paying for parking is a stretch for him.

It's a well-kept secret in the TV/movie/streaming content legal world that (a) attorneys are business people and (b) they need to be paid to continue to be attorneys.

One of Connecticut's best known criminal defense attorneys recently wrote this in his weekly *New Haven Register* column: "Almost every lawyer I know is struggling to keep the lights on these days." That's Norm Pattis, and while he is somewhat exaggerating (the column was an attempt to explain the appeal of Donald Trump) and "struggling" is a very, very subjective term, he does underscore the much overlooked truism of the practice of law: lawyers need to be paid like everyone else who works for a living.

No one ever saw Perry Mason or any of the guys from *LA Law* scrambling to pay the bills. As a matter of fact, Della Street seemed remarkably well paid for a 1950's solo practitioner's legal assistant. Popular culture portrayals of lawyers almost never even hint at the business side of practice, other than, for example, *The Lincoln Lawyer's* brief, eupehmistic reference to the absence of a Mr. Green, meaning, the client hasn't paid. Other examples are almost universally about a poor but noble lawyer working a case without hope of payment.

Attorneys are not like doctors, they are not locked into a "specialization." In fact, Bar Association rules in most states prohibit attorneys from saying they specialize in or are an expert in any one area of the law.

Do you know what the equivalent title for Neurologist/Oncologist/Orthopedic is in the law?

Attorney.

Attorneys are taught to think like an attorney – that's it, that's what law school is all about, thinking. Studying for the Bar exam means studying every aspect of the law. Torts, Bankruptcy, Easements, Constitutional, Criminal. Everything. And then thinking it all through.

When you pass the Bar, you're a lawyer. There are no restrictions on the license, no restrictions on what you can do with it. The medical equivalent is like your cardiologist removing a mole from your back (this happened to my husband, actually).

Here's something that shouldn't be a surprise to anyone but frequently is: lawyers have student loans, lawyers need to eat, lawyers can accept any case they want as long as there's no looming conflict of interest. Not all lawyers are rich.

Most lawyers stay with what they know and are comfortable with. It's smart, minimizes potential problems, allows for real expertise (although, per Bar rules, no one can really say they're an expert) and rapport with the court and "the other side."

When lawyers go "outside the box" they usually do so for one of two reasons: a friend or relative needs help; or, they need the retainer to keep the lights on. They are especially apt to do the second if they think they can easily stray into the new area of law without any challenges.

In other words, they are more likely to stray into what I do, help homeowners with foreclosure, than to take on, say, a civil rights action. Which is, of course, a misconception that can only arise when a practitioner is unfamiliar with handling foreclosure actions.

The problem is foreclosure law, like bankruptcy and a host others, looks very much on the surface like an orderly, procedure-driven process. A, B, C ... Z, keep the house.

This would be great if it were true. But it's not. Foreclosure defense is fraught with little hiccups and steep, nasty pitfalls that don't show up in the manuals and guides – on-line or off. The only way to know where they are is to do it every day for hundreds of clients in a hundred different scenarios with scores of banks, mortgage companies, and lawyers on the other side. That doesn't include knowing the judges, clerks, and mediators in each court.

The learning curve in foreclosure court is steep, the timeline is restrictive, no one should go through it with the additional stress of watching their attorney catch up on the fly.

§

A staple of the legal thriller – for movies and television, from *Anatomy of a Murder* through *Legally Blonde, The Good Wife* and everything in between - is the client who doesn't exactly give all the facts to her attorney.

That's fiction and it's fun and without that plot mechanism a great many movies and series just do not work. The totally honest, up front client is not the stuff that makes a good legal thriller.

I, however, deal strictly in reality and here it is:

Facts are facts. Some are good, some are bad. I talk to a lot of people about the facts of their situation. I have to deal 100% in facts to competently represent someone.

I can tell when someone is giving me the good facts while trying to "spin" the bad. They talk to me like they are making their best argument to a judge. I get complicated answers to simple questions.

When I notice this, I explain that regardless of the case, the easily winnable or not-a-chance case and everything else, there are always good and there are always bad facts. Always. I need to know them all.

I spoke on and off for several months with a homeowner about her foreclosure situation. Despite several phone conversations and email exchanges, the homeowner never mentioned the home was a condo and in addition to the mortgage company foreclosing, the condo association was also foreclosing. That's a very important fact. I'm not sure why she did not reveal this to me. It isn't the kind of bad fact that a homeowner doesn't want to admit to (like falling behind on a mortgage because of a gambling problem). By the time she told me this, it was almost too late.

I'm OK with bad facts. There are always bad facts. I can handle bad facts. There was that time that I learned *IN THE MIDDLE OF A DEPOSITION* that my client had been arrested for cocaine possession. That's a bad fact. But I have a great poker face, and I can handle it, I just really prefer no surprises.

No client has all good facts. Those clients don't exist.

Don't hesitate to recognize what might be your bad facts and trust your lawyer with them. It's how you and your lawyer handle your bad facts that will save you.

After all, as that professor said, neither of you want to end up in a case book or a legal thriller.

2. Early Cases

The debt business looked completely different when I first opened my solo practice than it does today. That was 2006, the height of the real estate market. We didn't know it was the height of the real estate market at the time, though. We were all riding the wave. It was two years after I bought my first home. I was still reading the real estate listings in my area to see what my home compared to, to verify that we got a good deal, so I could measure how much equity we had already earned based on comparable home prices.

One phenomenon that existed in 2006 and even into early 2008 was that people would use their home equity to pay off debt. They literally used their homes as ATM machines to withdraw cash. If the house was worth $250,000 but you only owed $200,000, you had $50,000 in cash value, in theory, to tap into.

Many, many people borrowed from this equity to remodel kitchens and perform other home improvements, go on vacations, pay off car loans and pay off other debt like credit card debt.

When homeowners had unpaid credit card debt and found themselves subject to collection lawsuits, they would go to their bank or to a mortgage broker and borrow money from their home equity to pay off their debt. The lawsuits would then be dropped. Easy.

When the market turned and the economy crashed, home values went down and there was no home equity left to tap into. In addition, there were no more funds to borrow. Lending simply dried up for a while there.

Just before the crash, I noticed a new "player" on the scene. The company was called Scopes & Associates, LLC, a debt buyer. That means someone set up a "limited liability company" (LLC) and started purchasing portfolios of unpaid credit card debt. Debt buying has been happening since the dawn of time, and I was very familiar with the concept, and was focusing on representing consumers being sued by debt buyers.

When I started seeing Scopes & Associates cases on the docket and getting calls from consumers being sued by Scopes, I took it in stride.

We consumer protection attorneys are a small group and we communicate often with each other. Just around the time I started my solo practice I noticed another Connecticut attorney had recently joined the National Association of Consumer Advocates. I must have logged onto the Association site to change my contact information and noticed an attorney named Henry Drummond was a new member. He listed credit card collection defense and debt collection harassment matters as the two main areas of his practice, same as me. I gave him a call.

Henry had worked for the State of Connecticut for 30 years and when he retired he put out a shingle. I'm not sure how he got involved in consumer protection matters but he seemed to have a lot of insight into how the cases typically went and how to help people with them. While I had more technology know-how (Henry was still using a typewriter!), Henry had better perspective on these cases and even talked me off the figurative ledge when I had made a big mistake in a case.

After working for 30 years for the State and knowing he had a secure pension, he was able to take more of a "who gives a crap" approach when dealing with our opponents. That is, he could afford to go big with his demands.

He and I started dealing with Scopes & Associates at around the same time and so we compared notes. I called Henry one day and I remember asking him, "Is it me or is this guy Matthew Brady a jerk to everyone?" Matthew was the attorney who represented Scopes in all the court cases that were filed. Henry said that Matthew was probably just testing me, that he had dealt with him a few times already and he was only a jerk the first time.

We are lucky here in Connecticut that we have an online docket system that allows you to look up a lot of information from different angles. For example, if you want to look up all the cases filed by Scopes & Associates, you just go to the "party name search" page and type "Scopes" into the name search field, and hit enter. If you want to see all the cases an attorney is handling, you look up his bar number and then do a bar number search for cases.

I started there. I found that not only did Matthew represent Scopes & Associates, but another company called Hillsboro.

I called Henry. I asked if he knew what Hillsboro was. Henry said yes, another company Matthew represents. Henry said he asked Matthew about the two companies and Matthew said his wife owned them.

There are essentially three remedies for collecting on a judgment in Connecticut: bank execution, wage execution and property lien. If Scopes got a judgment against a consumer for an unpaid credit card account balance, it could put a property lien on the consumer's property. If the consumer did not pay that lien, Scopes could start a foreclosure action to foreclose on that lien. I didn't notice Scopes filing any foreclosure actions, though. I noticed that Hillsboro, the company supposedly owned by his wife, was only filing foreclosure actions.

I went back to the "party name search" page of the online docket and found the name of someone who was being foreclosed on by Hillsboro. Let's say it's John Smith.

I then went back to the "party name search" page and typed in John Smith. The search would reveal all cases filed against John Smith, and in his case, he had first been sued by Scopes. I noticed that almost everyone who was being sued in foreclosure by Hillsboro also had been sued by Scopes on an unpaired credit card account balance. Everyone in foreclosure with Hillsboro had an outstanding judgment obtained by Scopes.

I wrote down a few names and went to look at files at the court.

I pulled the Scopes v. John Smith and the Hillsboro v. John Smith files which showed how the scheme would go:

Scopes, represented by Matthew Brady, sued Smith for an unpaid credit card balance and obtained a judgment against him, let's say for $10,000.

Scopes then transferred or assigned that judgment to Hillsboro.

Hillsboro, now the owner of the judgment obtained by Scopes, filed a judgment lien on Smith's property records.

Hillsboro then commenced a foreclosure suit against Smith.

The goal with collection suits and foreclosure suits is to get paid. Scopes wanted to get paid. After the Scopes judgments were made payable to Hillsboro, Hillsboro wanted to get paid. Sometimes it would get paid- sometimes people did come up with the money and pay off the judgments. However, Scopes and Hillsboro came on the scene at the wrong time. Most of the cases were brought starting in late 2007. Bad timing since after 2007 tapping into home equity to pay off credit card debt became increasingly more difficult due to the housing bubble bursting and decline in home values.

To compensate, Matthew did what I believed to be unthinkable for a lawyer.

I learned a little more about Matthew during the height of the Scopes era. First, it turns out he, not his wife, was the owner of Scopes. He never admitted to being the sole owner, he always claimed there were other owners but he never gave up any names.

I never understood the secrecy. I learned that Matthew, even though a licensed attorney, worked most of his career in property development. I met another attorney who had traveled in the same social circles as Matthew over the years and she said he was always kind of a jerk to everyone. When I told her he had started purchasing old credit card debt and suing people and foreclosing on people, she wasn't surprised.

He and I were talking before a hearing one day and he told me about his young daughters. He was in his late fifties and so, like most parents with young kids, complained about how much work they were (but was also very proud of them). I tend to wonder what motivates people to do what they do-- especially if they choose willingly to foreclose on peoples' homes-- so I started to put together a theory about Matthew and why he changed courses in 2007 and got into the debt-buying and lawyering business after all those years in property development. It started to make sense when I learned about his young children.

Brady appeared to be violating federal law and much of the lawyers' code of conduct, in the process, however.

Here's how it worked.

Scopes would obtain a judgment like that $10,000 against John Smith. Scopes would assign the judgment to Hillsboro. Matthew's signature was on most, if not all, of the assignments from Scopes to Hillsboro. Hillsboro would place a lien, signed by Matthew, on the defendant's property. Then Hillsboro, represented by Matthew, would file a foreclosure suit to foreclose on the judgment lien.

There's nothing wrong with any of this – so far. But if the person couldn't pay Scopes when that suit was brought, there wasn't much chance that they could pay Hillsboro when the foreclosure was brought. Which meant that Matthew wasn't getting paid.

Here's where it got dirty. Matthew would get impatient and go back into the Scopes cases and file requests for bank executions or wage executions with the court. Scopes had the right to do this, but not if it no longer owned the judgment. A classic double-dip.

The vast majority of Hillsboro foreclosure cases were based on Scopes judgments. The document that allowed Hillsboro to foreclose on a Scopes judgment was an absolute assignment, that is, the document stated that Scopes assigned *ALL ITS RIGHTS* to the judgment to Hillsboro. This document was never filed in the Scopes files with the court, however. The court had no way to detect the scheme of Scopes asking for remedies it *no longer* had the right to request since it had assigned judgment to Hillsboro.

Consumers therefore found themselves fighting off a Hillsboro foreclosure case at the same time they were fighting off having their wages garnished or their bank accounts frozen in the Scopes case.

In addition to violating our federal debt collection laws, because Scopes was doing things it no longer had the right to do when it sought bank and wage executions on judgments it no longer owned, Matthew was engaging in acts I believed were in violation of the lawyers' code of ethics. The least of which was when he failed to inform the court in the Scopes cases that the judgments had been completely assigned over to Hillsboro. If the judges and clerks had figured out Scopes no longer had the right to collect on those judgments, they would never have issued those executions.

I was appalled. This was ballsy - to me it was blatant violations of the debt collection laws and our code of conduct which requires lawyers to act with candor to the court. It insulted me that he was doing this and the court couldn't see it. So I started reaching out to the people being foreclosed on by Hillsboro.

Lawyers in Connecticut are allowed to write letters to potential clients. The code of conduct dictates certain language we need to include in these letters and instructs us to stamp "Advertising Material" in red on the envelope and on the top of the letter. I followed all these rules. I also really wanted to get the attention of the people I wrote to because I could see in black and white that they were victims of the scheme.

Instead of the vanilla language I usually put in the letters, I included a sentence or two that went something like this: "Please contact me to discuss what I believe may be violations of federal law by Scopes and its attorney." I received several responses and was retained by several people.

Here's where the story goes sideways. One of the people I sent the letters to called Matthew's office, told them they received my letter, and gave it to him. Matthew then filed a grievance with the state Bar against *me*.

On top of that, a few months later I came home from vacation to papers in my door: Matthew was SUING me!

I explain this to people like this: "Well, I was trying to put him out of business so he tried to put me out of business."

I proceeded to defend the people who hired me and to prosecute the cases I had brought against Matthew for the Scopes bank execution/Hillsboro foreclosure misconduct. I didn't see Matthew that often but I noticed that he looked very different each time. Age was catching up to him quickly.

I then wanted to take his deposition in some of the cases my clients had brought against him. He was away in California for an extended period around this time, however. I didn't quite understand how he could go across the country for months at a time when he had so many active cases in suit in Connecticut. He had associates and outside counsel helping of course, but the timing seemed strange. I hoped that he wasn't there because one of his kids was sick and that is where they had to go for treatment.

We took the depositions via video feed.

I hired a good attorney to help me defend the grievance Matthew had filed against me. My attorney managed to get hearings in the matter delayed quite a bit and in the interim, three grievances were filed against Matthew for similar conduct-- one by a defendant, one by a fellow consumer attorney representing defendants against Scopes and Hillsboro and one by a judge. Matthew was in trouble. The grievance against me-- based on the language in my letter suggesting Scopes and its attorney may have violated federal law-- seemed small now in light of the three pending against him.

My attorney's strategy to have the claim against me be overshadowed by all the claims brought against Matthew (which validated my suspicions that he may have engaged in violations of law) worked. I agreed to take a 2-hour ethics course and the claims against me were dropped. Matthew took a reprimand. That basically means one strike in a two-strike system; the next wrong move and he could get suspended or disbarred.

Matthew didn't look good at the grievance hearing.

The suit he brought against me was still pending. I had to file a claim with my malpractice policy to get an attorney paid for by my insurance. My attorney did a good job in that matter too, dragging it out. Finally we heard Matthew's demand: $15,000. My policy was willing to pay $10,000. My husband said, "Let's just cough up the additional $5,000 and get this over with."

Of course, that went against every fiber of my being, but I agreed and let my lawyer know. Maybe my insurance carrier just wanted to know I cared and when I made that offer they came up to $15,000 and the deal was sealed. Case dropped.

Three months later Matthew was dead.

It all made sense. He started the scheme when he got a diagnosis of prostate cancer. He had recently married a woman very much his junior and they had two young daughters. He was building something for them that would produce a stream of income after he was gone: payments on judgments obtained in court, payments when homeowners tried to avoid foreclosures of those judgment liens, and if the properties were foreclosed on, then a portfolio of real estate in Connecticut.

He didn't care how he had to do it, thus the violations of law and of the code of conduct. Medical treatment in California may have bought him some time. He didn't have time to follow the rules.

When I tell people this story and that Matthew died, I say, "See what happens when you sue me!" I know that's terrible and of course I'm joking.

The aftermath of his death was not pretty. His daughters lost their father and I know what that is like. I had heard that he and his own father had been very close, best friends even. I found out that just about a week after Matthew died, his father died. It's like one of those stories about the elderly couple who die together because they can't live without the other, or like Carrie Fisher and Debbie Reynolds.

Is the moral of this story that Matthew was just another lawyer who gave lawyers a bad name? No, that's not it. Matthew did what he had to do to fight for his family, but that couldn't have been 100% his motivation. After all, people who are honest in life don't usually turn dishonest even for noble causes. Was it for me to be taught a lesson? I learned not to be so shocked by the bad behavior of others, even of lawyers, and I'm a little more careful when I draft letters to potential clients now. When I step back to see where Matthew's passing affected the debt buying business, how cases are brought, how consumers are treated along the way by the creditors and the courts, I don't see how any of it has changed. Scopes and Hillsboro sure lost steam when Matthew died. I think the lesson is that the only way to change the system for the better is when fewer people are prosecuting the cases and pursing the consumer for payment. Basically, it will stop only when they all die out.

§

The best tool we have here in Connecticut is that our Judicial Branch posts most court information online. Case names, party names, their attorneys and any recent activity in such cases as credit card collection cases, foreclosures and personal injury matters appear online. You can search by docket number if you know it or by party name. When someone calls me and leaves their name and tells me they're being sued or they're in foreclosure, I will look up their case to get an idea of what is going on before calling them back.

The day before my 40th birthday I received a call from a potential client who said she had a foreclosure problem. Big understatement. When I went online to check the case, she was four days from a foreclosure auction due to unpaid property taxes. I called her back. What is your plan for getting your taxes paid and your house back in good standing? Do you have income, can you get the $35,000 from somewhere? Well, she explained, she had been in a terrible accident a few years earlier and was completely disabled. Are you receiving disability income? No, I never wanted to admit that I was completely disabled, but I guess that was a mistake, she explained. I said that if she had disability income, or if she at least was in the process of applying for disability benefits with the Social Security Administration, I may be able to buy her more time. She also claimed she had made a $5,000 payment toward her taxes AND was on a payment plan with the town so she didn't understand why they were moving forward with her foreclosure.

"How did you get my name?" I finally asked.

"Well, I looked online for a lawyer and called Attorney Neil Atlas in West Hartford." Oh boy. I know what this meant. In the fall of 2008, I represented a woman whose foreclosure case had been pending since 2002. That's right, 2002.

Long story short, that homeowner was just a couple of weeks away from losing title to her house through a process called strict foreclosure, which is what happens when you have no equity in your home- you owe as much as or more than your property is worth, and there is no auction, the title to the property just passes back to the bank on a certain day set by the court. The court had a mediation program but it was supposed to only be available to homeowners whose cases commenced after July 2008. But I knew all the players and ins and outs of the program and figured if I could get her case into mediation, we could work something out with her bank. By the time she retained me, she had already had her entire church call our local senator and the CEO of her mortgage lender. She had primed the pump; when I ultimately got her out of foreclosure, I didn't feel like I could take much of the credit.

But Attorney Neil Atlas, an old-timer who was representing the bank in that case, complimented me on how I helped the client and how I obtained the result. In his eyes, if there was an impossible case, it should be referred to me.

UGH. I double checked the new client's case information online. We were lucky. The town to whom the client owed back taxes was being represented by an attorney I had dealt with before. She was nice and respected me, and put some thought into the foreclosures—didn't treat homeowners like just another number. She saw the benefit to giving homeowners more time, a rarity in foreclosures in our corner of the world. I knew she would work with me and get me any documents or other information I needed if I agreed to represent this client.

Before agreeing to meet with the client, I must have told her at least five times that I was not a miracle worker but I had a couple of ideas on how I could buy her some time. The best I could do for her, and the best a lawyer who helps homeowners in foreclosure can do for their clients, is buy them more time. Another two weeks, a month, three months could change everything. I also agreed to meet with her only if she brought all her paperwork, including proof that she paid the town $5,000 earlier in the year and that she had made payments to the town toward her back taxes. She agreed.

I wasn't sure that I really wanted to represent her. She came across as a bit nuts. I think a bad car accident jars someone and they are never really the same. I heard hints of conspiracy theories in her explanation of what had led her to this point and I didn't want to commit to her and file an appearance in her file if she was totally hopeless.

I quoted her an hourly rate and set up an appointment for her to come to my office two days later, two days before her foreclosure auction.

At two o'clock on the first day of my 40th year, Mary walked through the door. It was late in the afternoon and I was feeling sick. The day before, my 40th, I began to come down with a cold. I wasn't feeling so bad that I needed to take the next day off, and knowing Mary's situation was time sensitive, to say the least, I could not postpone that appointment.

It was not too uncommon for someone seeking my assistance with their financial troubles to walk in with a folder or bag of mail and papers they hadn't opened or ever looked at. Mary's were a mix of unopened and wrinkled from exposure to moisture and moldy. I sifted through it all looking for evidence that she had indeed been making regular payments to the town and for proof of the $5,000 payment earlier in the year. If I could refute the claim by the bank that she failed to make payments under the payment agreement, I would have at least one basis to make a motion to postpone the foreclosure auction. I did also see a doctor's note with various dates from months and years past, but she had already told me she hadn't applied for Social Security benefits yet so I didn't bother reading them. I was not about to try to determine if she would indeed be given full disability benefits – I knew someone who could work with her on an application and would leave that to him.

She hadn't really brought me proof of regular payments to the town, but she did bring a carbon copy of a $5,000 cashier's check made out to the town the previous June. That was good, but it turns out the town's attorney, who I'd known to generally be a straight shooter, had not given it to the town nor had she returned it to my client. For three months after tendering the check to the town, my client believed she had made a sufficient payment to get back on track. In September, the town made a motion for judgment and only that day returned the check to her. Not fair and not cool, I thought, and so I intended to put that in my motion to extend the foreclosure sale.

My plan at that point was to file a motion to open the foreclosure judgment for Mary. I told her I'd get started on the motion and asked her to meet me at the court at 11 am the next day. I'm not sure why I didn't at that point take the $1000 in cash she brought to the office as a retainer. I took $200 for the time we spent that day and told her to bring more the next day depending on how much work I'd need to do.

I woke up even sicker than the day before but knew I had to get to the court with Mary's motion. I received an email from the town's attorney with a tax payment history attached and saw that Mary had not made payments with any regularity to the town. I also didn't see the $5000 payment anywhere and thought I could use that to request more time.

With a box of tissues and a bag of lozenges in hand, I headed to the office. I cut and pasted Mary's case name into a standard motion, changed the details to suit her situation, and emailed it to myself.

The court has what they call a Court Service Center near the clerk's office with tables, phones, a copier and fax machine, a few computers with printers, and an information desk. Many courts do not have very nice service centers, they lack amenities, and are small – as small as a broom closet.

This court, though, had an excellent center with several work stations, some large tables where you can meet with clients, a large wall of forms and informational booklets, and an information desk staffed with at least two clerks, one bilingual in Spanish and one in Polish, since, although called New Britain, this town has a large Polish population.

I logged into one of the computers and printed out the motion. Then I called the client to make sure she was on her way. She was. I then started drafting up an affidavit for her to sign, listing all the efforts she had made to pay her taxes, including the $5000 payment that the town's lawyer unfairly held and did not give to the town.

My phone rang again. It was Mary, she said she got into a fender bender. It was noon. She said she was OK, that her car was OK, and she was still on her way. I wanted to put my head down on the desk and take a nap.

Within the hour, she arrived and sat down next to me at the work station. I smelled alcohol on her breath. Oh great. This is what I needed. I went over her affidavit with her, she agreed with the facts as I spelled them out, and she signed it.

I then told her I was ready to file her motion and she needed to pay the $125 filing fee to the court. She looked in her purse for her money and realized she left her money in her car. I told her to go get it and as I watched her walk out the door, wondered what the chances were that she'd come back.

A few minutes later she called. This time she locked her keys in her car. Are you kidding me? She had called AAA and said they'd be there soon. I crossed my fingers as I hung up that she was telling the truth. Still feeling miserable, I took this opportunity to call the town's lawyer and let her know I was at the courthouse ready to file the motion. She had no good explanation for not giving the town the $5,000, but said she was glad Mary finally got an attorney.

Mary did finally come back into the court, and I asked her for the money. She pulled out what looked like the same bank envelope from the day before, but it had much less than $800 in it. She found $125 but I could tell there was not much left. I had her sign a retainer agreement with me but it was clear she didn't have enough to cover all my time plus the court fee. I think she paid me another $200.

We filed the motion and waited. As it was the day before the foreclosure auction, there would be no hearing. The clerk took the motion to the judge on duty on Friday afternoon for review. The judge had the sole discretion to cancel or postpone the sale or to let it go forward. It was about 2 pm.

35

I had run out of tissues and lozenges and I hadn't eaten lunch yet. I'm not one of those dedicated lawyers who skips meals and loses sleep to work. I always break for lunch and leave the office by 6 pm, and rarely bring work home. Even if I hadn't been sick, I would have been suffering at this point in the day. But I was assured the motion was on the judge's desk and so I didn't want to leave. For some reason, the little cafeteria in the court house was closed that day.

Mary and I waited in the hallway outside the clerk's office. She fell asleep. I used the ladies' room and wished I was home in bed. When I came back, she was slouched in the corner on a bench with her head against the wall. Her posture reminded me of a homeless person. And she had started to drool. At 4 pm, I went into the clerk's office again to check on the status of the motion. Denied. I woke Mary up, told her the bad news, and walked her to her car.

There is one last ditch chance for a homeowner who loses their house in a foreclosure sale. You have 30 days to "redeem" the property, so if you can pay the debt plus the foreclosure fees, you can get your house back. Mary said she'd try to get the money together and get back to me.

Mary was lucky. That winter was the snowiest winter we'd had in years. On the day a few weeks later that the foreclosure sale was supposed to be approved, I trudged out to my car in about 4 inches of slush, more thick snowflakes coming down, and headed to court. I had checked several times that morning to verify whether the hearing to approve the sale was delayed or postponed, but there was no indication on the court's website that there were any snow delays.

I left extra early and sat next to the lawyer for the town. Lawyers and other litigants started to fill the courtroom for the call of all the cases. The town's lawyer and I were waiting for the committee, the lawyer assigned by the court to conduct the foreclosure sale. It was her motion and she'd need to be there to ask the judge to approve the sale and to order payment of her fees for her services. I had spoken to her the day before, a Sunday, and told her I'd be at the hearing. She verified she'd be there too.

But she wasn't when the hearing started at 9:30 and the judge came out and started to hear motions. At 10, the lawyer for the town and I were going through our files looking for the committee attorney's phone numbers. I had her office number but did not have her cell number. Well, I did have it, but I couldn't read my own writing and got a wrong number. I guessed at the correct number and finally reached her.

"Oh," she said, "I can't go out in this weather. I asked the clerk to have the judge just take the motion on the papers."

"Really?" I said.

"I would have called you but I figured you were in court," was her reasoning.

"My work number is a cell phone, you really should have called me. I'm going to object to your motion now," I said.

I went back into the courtroom and delivered the news to the lawyer for the town. Her jaw dropped. Our case was called, I

37

introduced myself for the record and informed the judge that I was now objecting to the approval of the foreclosure sale because the committee was not there.

The court agreed and said the committee could ask the motion to be heard at a later date. This lucky delay was good news for Mary.

Mary never did come up with the money to save the house and she stopped responding to my calls. The sale was eventually approved and the attorney for the buyers contacted me asking whether she'd be cleaning out her possessions. I still did had not heard from her.

One Monday morning a couple of weeks later, the attorney for the buyers emailed me asking whether I knew if my client was in Florida. He said he'd learned that she had been arrested, and that I should view the attachment to the email. I opened it up and it was a mug shot taken a few weeks before in Tampa. I let out a big sigh and said, "Poor Mary" out loud as I recognized a scruffier, more tired looking image of the woman who had sat in my office surrounded by moldy, wrinkled paper just a few weeks before.

I replied to the email that it was indeed my client, and thought to myself, the week can only get better when it starts out with someone emailing you mug shots of your client.

3. Court

All my friends and family know I'm a lawyer. Often when I get together with them, they ask how work is going. Some don't exactly know what my job is like day to day, and will ask if I go to court. I say yes, but I always explain that it's not like on *Law and Order*. Well, sometimes, rarely but sometimes, it is like *Law and Order*, and can even be better than *Law and Order* (you really can't make up the stuff that happens in court).

But I usually try to explain that my court experiences are mostly just meetings with the client, a court mediator and a lawyer who represents a mortgage lender. There are occasional trials. Trials are sometimes like you see on TV. Don't let any lawyer tell you that they haven't adopted some courtroom skills or learned how to think more analytically from reading a John Grisham novel or from watching scripted trials on TV or in the movies (think Matthew McConaughey in *A Time to Kill* or *The Lincoln Lawyer*…)

If they deny it, they either have never read Grisham or have stayed away from law shows or movies as if they were a member of a sequestered jury. One of the earliest trials I ever sat in on was probably as good or better than any scene in *Law and Order*. It was when I worked for the blind attorney who represented my state's child protective services agency. The trial was to justify the removal of a 2 year-old boy from parents who were accused of abusing him.

No jury, just a judge, a lawyer for each parent, a lawyer for the child, my boss representing the Department of Children & Families, her guide dog and me.

The boy had sustained a deep cut to his eye, just under his eyebrow. The hospital called the authorities when they treated the wound. The parents said he fell off a chair while eating, bringing a ceramic mug down with him, which they say broke and cut his eye.

The ophthalmic surgeon who examined him (and who was a witness at the trial) said that that story didn't match the injury, which was a deep cut in a straight line, and there was no sign the boy had fallen on his hands and knees, which typically bear evidence of an attempt to break a fall.

The interesting part was that the surgeon was a hostile witness— he resented being subpoenaed to testify on behalf of the State, which took time out of his day. He was impatient with the process, and it was difficult at first for the attorney I worked for to elicit testimony from him. He stated the facts as he remembered them and from his reports of the injury (luckily the child did not lose vision). He was not very interesting or compelling.

Then the parents' attorney started to cross examine the doctor. This is where I learned that less is more when it comes to cross-examination. The parents tried to get the doctor to admit the injury could have occurred as they had described. At this the doctor seemed to come out of his shell- it was if he started to recall what it was like examining the little kid with the deep cut, what it would have taken to give the boy that injury and how close they came to blinding him in that eye.

The cross examination only made it worse for the parents because the doctor could tell that their explanation did not make sense and he began to eagerly explain what he believe happened—he said the injury was so deep, and there seemed to be no defensive injuries, that it was as if the boy had been taken completely off guard. That the only way the injury could have occurred was if someone threw something at him with such velocity at close range—like throwing a Frisbee. Only the object was probably a plate that broke when it hit him or was already broken.

By the time the doctor was done testifying, he was an engaged and angry witness, indignant that anyone would ever treat a child in this way. The transformation was amazing, and the parents were toast.

It was better than TV. My own courtroom skills were developed in those days working for the blind attorney because it was part of my job to tell her what was going on.

She would ask about the judge's expression and body language, she would have me describe the parents, their attorneys, anyone else in the court room. She would be busy concentrating on her direct examination, which she often memorized, and making sure all the necessary evidence was entered in the record and nothing important missed. My job was to keep an eye on everything else.

Sometimes she would turn to me after asking most of her questions of a witness and ask what the judge was doing; I remember specifically one time telling her he was sitting way back in his chair and looking at the ceiling. "No more questions, your honor," was her response.

Another trial was opposing the emancipation petition of a 16-year-old in the care of the state child protective services agency. The agency did not believe she should be emancipated, they were worried she didn't have the resources to support herself and finish high school.

She was a sophisticated kid, though, and made a good case: she rented a room in an apartment, had a job at a local fast food restaurant and was maintaining good grades. At a point late in the trial, she took out a plastic case, took something out of it and put it in her mouth. It was her retainer—she had had braces on her teeth and was still wearing retainers.

I turned to my boss and said, "Um, she just put in her retainer. I wonder who is paying for her medical and dental." My boss used this information, asked her where she would get her medical and dental insurance if she left the state's care, and she said she didn't know, she didn't have enough hours at her job to get medical and dental there.

Result: petition denied. I was happy my observation skills had lent some value.

Once I became a lawyer, I started having my own court experiences. I had observed plenty and having worked for the blind attorney gave me enough exposure to hearings and trials to last a lifetime. I was probably the only one in my law school class who could honestly say that if they never saw the inside of a courtroom again they wouldn't miss it.

It turns out I took a job that required litigation. That's the lawyer term for "I have to go to court a lot." My early court appearances were almost out-of-body experiences. I had practiced for each court appearance but was so nervous at first I felt detached. I felt like it was an act.

Whoever said there was nothing wrong with "faking it until you make it" nailed it. That was essentially what I was doing- using what I had learned in my non-lawyer life and transferring those skills to my lawyer life.

For example, in college I studied French. I lived in France for a year too, studying there. I observed a phenomenon when I was learning a new language I called "the 3-second rule," which is where someone says something to you in the foreign language, it takes your brain 3 seconds to comprehend it and formulate a response, but by that time the person who asked you the question has figured out you are American and starts speaking English to you... which is not what you want when you're trying to function 100% in the new language.

I developed a skill of starting to ask a question about what the person had said while my brain processed what they said and formulated an appropriate response. This prevented the person I was talking with from treating me like an American they thought didn't understand the language.

When in court if I don't understand something, if something the judge or opposing counsel or witness says isn't clear, I do not hesitate to ask for clarification, to admit that maybe I missed something and need clarification or need something repeated, etc.

Nothing wrong with this, and it sometimes buys me the time my brain needs to process an appropriate response to the situation, especially if things don't seem to be going my client's way. You get better at this and it makes the whole courtroom thing feel like less of an act after a while.

I'd like to think all my clients get a fair shot at their case when they are in court, but unfortunately judges are just not blank slates. Justice may be blind but judges are not: they come into their courtrooms with their own life experiences. When those experiences benefit my client, I don't complain, so I can't exactly complain when they do not benefit my client.

One of the most outrageous courtroom experiences I have had, which could have translated perfectly to television, was in a trial where I was defending a client against having to pay a large credit card debt.

It was not a jury trial, just a "court trial" which was heard only by a judge. My client's account had gone unpaid for many months, and his credit card company had sold off the account along with a portfolio of other unpaid credit card accounts to a debt buyer.

The plaintiff in the case was the debt buyer, and its lawyer proved to not exactly respect the typical courtroom decorum. Representing the plaintiff, he put on his case first. He called an employee of the debt buyer as his witness. After he questioned her, it was my turn to cross examine.

One question I always ask in these trials is how much her company paid for the account. This information is not relevant—I mean, I feel like it is, but technically it doesn't matter, her company bought the right to collect the entire balance, so it doesn't really matter how much the company paid.

The attorney for the debt buyer objected, we had a little back-and-forth about it and the judge permitted my question. Victory. But when the witness tried to answer how much the company paid for the account, she said she didn't know, it was hard to tell, she wasn't sure, there were different prices paid for different types of portfolios of accounts, whiffle-waffle, vagueness, etc.

During all this equivocation, the judge was looking down and taking notes. Suddenly, the witness answers with a number. My client taps me hard— "He just told her what to say." What? Apparently, the lawyer fed his witness the answer! I responded by saying, "Did your attorney just tell you what to say?" which got the judge to look up. I started, "Your honor…" but the judge said, "Move along counselor."

I couldn't believe it. I don't think I had ever heard of a lawyer feeding a witness answers *while on the stand*, right under the judge's nose.

Since there was no jury, and the judge was looking down, he got away with it. Unbelievable.

Lately my court experiences are dominated by attending foreclosure mediations. These are relatively casual but important events in my clients' cases.

They require the same steps as when you attend other court events such as motion hearings or trials: you have to get there a bit early, park, walk up to the court house (it's never a short walk), go through security (why does *EVERY* pair of my shoes set off the metal detector??) and then find where the mediation will be located.

The mediations can last from 5 minutes to an hour but are rarely contentious or stressful. That's why when my friends or family ask me about court, I make the point of making sure they don't think everything I do is out of *Law and Order*. I'm not sure why- court is a big deal for my clients. And it is a big deal for the status of and progress in my cases.

It's such a common part of my job now that going to court and speaking in front of judges and courtrooms full of people or advocating for my client in a foreclosure mediation have become routine, as routine as the aspects of anyone else's job. Maybe the next time someone asks me if I go to court and what that's like, I should respond, "Remember the O.J. trial? Just like that," just see their reaction.

§

I was lucky on my first job as a lawyer, really lucky. I had a lot of independence and it was interesting, two traits not common to the first-year associate experience. One day my boss said, "Let's look into the Fair Credit Reporting Act—find out everything you can about the credit bureaus and credit scores," and left me alone for three days.

I went right to the source—the websites for Equifax, Experian and Trans Union, the three major credit reporting agencies. I read and read and read, and followed link after link on their sites until I got an idea of what they were about, what those companies had to offer and what the purpose was of a credit report and a credit score.

Then I started meeting with potential clients who were having issues based on credit scores or inaccurate information on their credit reports. I met with one gentleman who had a *VERY* common name. If I told you his name was John Smith I wouldn't be violating any attorney-client confidences because how would you know which John Smith? That kind of common name.

This Smith was nearing retirement age, was in good financial health, was married, had a nice house but his credit report contained all kinds of junk. Accounts that were not his. Inquiries into his credit history that he had not initiated. Negative items up the wazoo. And he was frustrated. I told him that the law that protects people like him requires that he write a letter with a list of the credit items on his report that were not his and send it to each credit bureau via certified mail (so he could prove the bureaus received his reports, otherwise the bureaus would be tempted to just toss his letter in the trash before opening it… *60 Minutes* did a story on this a few years ago).

He said he had done that already a year or so before but it didn't help- the other John Smith's negative credit history was still blended with his. He was fed up. He shouldn't have to go through the process again. He was right.

The reason he shouldn't have to go through the process again is because the credit bureaus should be able to tell that the negative accounts did not belong to this John Smith. They both lived in the same state but not in the same town. But here's how it works: you have already experienced some of the problems if you've ever attempted to obtain your own credit report. You have to jump through multiple hoops to prove to the credit bureaus that you are who you say you are. If you attempt to obtain your credit report online, you have to pass a quiz of sorts- the bureau will ask you to identify the name of a street you live on or have lived on; you need to know the amount you pay on certain monthly bills such as your car payment, etc.

If you answer any of these questions incorrectly, you can't access your credit report online. This is good for you really, this way a stranger or ex-boyfriend will be less likely to be able to obtain a copy of your report behind your back.

It may, then, be somewhat hard to get a credit report. But it's not hard to report credit information to someone's credit file. John Smith experienced this- the OTHER John Smith's creditors reported that John Smith's information, but when it arrived at the credit bureaus, the name matched, the state of residence matched, and that was enough to blend, or "merge" as the term is used in the industry, his negative information with the other John Smith's.

Once he informed the bureaus that certain accounts weren't his, that should have corrected it. Sometimes, although it shouldn't, it takes more than one letter to get everything corrected. (Second and third letters to bureaus should acknowledge the information that has been corrected but clearly point out that there is still work to do.)

I wanted to help Mr. Smith. I was chomping at the bit to get my hands on this guy's credit reports and help him write that next dispute letter. But he just didn't have the patience for it, and we never heard back from him.

I've met with others since meeting Mr. Smith whose reports contain others' information. One more recent potential client had a name such as Martin Roberts. He thought his identity had been stolen because there were odd items and credit inquiries on his credit reports. There was also a line on his report saying, "also known as Robert Martins" or something similar. I have access to a program that allows me to search basic information about people by inputting name and address, or other personal identifying information. I use this program when I think someone's identity has been stolen or I'm trying to find someone who has moved and I need updated address information. I tried a few different searches and discovered that the Robert Martins whose name also appeared on his credit had almost the exact same birthdate *AND* several digits of his Social Security number were the same.

It's hard to get your own credit report, but it's not hard to be blended with someone else.

Take the case of Judy Thomas. She lived in Texas and discovered negative credit information on her credit report that was not hers. It belonged to a woman with a somewhat similar name, who also lived in Texas, but in another town. She disputed the information to the credit bureaus. It was not removed. She suffered harm in the form of the inability to obtain credit and other "adverse action", as it's called in the Fair Credit Reporting Act. As a result, she found her way to a consumer protection attorney who took on TransUnion, the company that would not un-mix her information from the other woman's. She won, and the verdict was a healthy one.

Why did she have to sue the credit bureau to get this fixed? I too was involved in protracted litigation against a credit bureau, Equifax. A consumer attorney in another state contacted our office while I was still working at Consumer Law Group. He had been retained by a client who lived a few towns over from our office and whose identity had been stolen, and asked us to be local counsel. The client had recently left military service after putting in 20 years. He was attempting to adjust to civilian life and work when he applied for credit and was denied. He didn't understand why, so he requested a copy of his credit report.

Equifax would not give him his credit report—he hadn't provided the personal information that matched the information in

Equifax's files so they did not want to release his report. He requested his reports from the other bureaus and they provided them so he could see the reason for the credit denial.

His report was a total mess! Multiple accounts that he did not open; multiple inquiries into his credit from places he did not apply for credit with; different addresses and name spellings. Clearly his identity had been taken over. He disputed these things with Experian and TransUnion and they were removed. But Equifax still wouldn't provide him a copy of his report so he couldn't see what Equifax had in its files on him.

Then he began receiving collection letters, then collection calls. Calls all day. Letter after letter. He would try to get as much information about each account in collection when he took the calls, but as soon as he couldn't provide the information his imposter had used to open the account, the creditors and collectors would stop talking to him . . . to protect the imposter's privacy!

He spent months trying to ascertain the extent of the use of his identity and the number and type of accounts opened in his name. He had boxes filled with letters from collectors, his responses (all sent via certified mail at about $5 per letter), and responses from Equifax to his attempts to obtain the information in its files so he could properly inform Equifax which accounts were his and which were not, as was his right under the Fair Credit Reporting Act.

Turns out the imposter had obtained a copy of his military ID card and used that to obtain a driver's license in my client's name and then went on a spending spree. I kid you not: two cars, a motorcycle, multiple credit cards, medical and dental care, apartment leases, cell phones and checking accounts.

The imposter moved from state to state doing damage for about a year before the client's efforts at explaining that the accounts were not opened by him and the creditors were being ripped off by this other guy to the tune of about $250,000 started to slow down the frenzy.

Finally, someone at an auto finance company who had lent the imposter the funds to purchase an SUV got it—they were talking to the real guy who wanted to help them find the crook and stop the bleeding. A sting was set up and the guy was caught.

The imposter was more than 10 years younger than my client and was barely literate. Credit applications the client obtained showed the imposter couldn't even spell John correctly (statistically not a good name if you want to avoid blended credit files and ID theft, apparently)- he had copies of checks signed 'Jonh'. You almost wanted to feel sorry for him.

Imagine, though, going through this Kafkaesque process where you know you are you but everyone you talk to denies you are you.

You are the good guy but the bad guy gets all the privacy protections- such as using a different address to apply for credit so that Equifax thinks the imposter's address is now your real address, and since you don't know the imposter's address you can't get *YOUR* own report. The other guy, simply by applying for credit with some of my client's personal information but with a new address, managed to convince Equifax that my client's real information was false. Thus, he was able to stymie everyone's efforts *for months* at stopping him.

The stress on the client, the lost hours and days at work, the tension every time the phone rang, drove my client to depression. Here was an extremely competent, sound and healthy guy who was reduced to getting therapy and a prescription for an anti-depressant. The stress even put his marriage at risk. He admitted to us one day that instead of getting ready for work, he found himself sitting in his closet with his gun in his hand. Fighting the corporate credit bureau machine had become too much.

I met with this client weekly throughout his case as we discovered new accounts that had been opened, as new collectors took over for old collectors on accounts we were aware of, and as we took painstaking steps to clear his credit.

Not only could he not apply for or obtain credit, he couldn't write checks or open a new bank account. The imposter had opened checking accounts and then bounced checks. Dishonored (or "bounced") checks go into a whole other parallel system of credit reporting just for bank accounts. You may not know the major check verification systems by name but you may see Telecheck or Chex Systems equipment or logos at the registers at most major retailers. If you write a check at a store, you might see the clerk run it through a scanner to determine if that check is likely to clear. Negative information about my client was also recorded by these companies so he was virtually paralyzed financially.

So, what happened? We had to file a lawsuit against Equifax and three of the other recalcitrant creditors who failed to believe that my client *DIDN'T DO IT*. I can't remember who settled out first, but once parties pay and get out of the case, it leaves fewer defendants to share the same amount of blame. By settling, the client was compensated; part of those settlement discussions included the defendants claiming they had no systems for preventing this kind of thing from happening and acted as though it were going to be a priority to do something about that.

We weren't going to hold our breath on that one. Often when these cases settle there is no apology; indeed, typical language in settlement agreements includes wording to the effect that the defendant admits no liability and no liability should be assumed from the fact that the party agreed to a settlement. Scandals involving the credit bureaus continue to occur. It helped a little here that the attorney for Equifax seemed genuinely concerned with the role her client played in my client's hardship. The closest he got to satisfaction at the end of case, though, was being handed a corrected copy of his Equifax report.

§

Another interesting and telling experience I had with a client was another blended file. I don't recall this one being too difficult to fix. I gained insight, however, into how much stock the average person puts into his or her credit score.

This client's credit information was blended with his sister's information—this made sense in a few ways. First, they were in business together. Second, they were close in age and had had addresses in common, such as when they were in college and both lived at home. Also, it was common before the 1980s for a parent to obtain Social Security numbers for children at the same time, so often those numbers would be close in sequence. (After reading about Mr. Smith above, you can imagine the issues twins and fathers and sons who have the same name have with merged or blended credit files.)

This client's issue was that he wanted to purchase a home and he was concerned about his credit score. The problem with him was he was keeping an eye on his credit score even while we were still in the process of disputing items on his report that were not his and waiting for the credit bureaus' responses.

The defining moment for me came when he called me one day and exclaimed, "My credit score went down 14 points since yesterday!" I calmed him and responded that you can't watch your score every day; it's like watching the stock market. Also, although the algorithms used to calculate credit scores are secret, we know enough to know that scores are somewhat fluid- if his score went down in one day, others' scores probably also went down.

I could tell in a moment that for him it wasn't about needing a good score to get the best mortgage interest rate, it was about what his credit score said about him as a person. I heard myself say, "You know, your score is not your adult grade."

He asked me what I meant, and I recalled the episode of *The Simpsons* where the teachers are all on strike so there's no school for days. Bart, of course was thrilled. Lisa, however, was beside herself. She was bored, but more notably she was missing something. Marge asked her to set the table, and when she was done, Marge thanked her. Lisa cried out, "But Mom, how did I do? GRADE ME! Evaluate me!"

This is what the client was looking to his credit score to accomplish for him: he wanted to know how he was doing as an adult. I pointed out that when we're in school, we're constantly being graded. But when we get out in the world, there's much less structure in this regard. If you don't have a job that evaluates you regularly, you might turn to credit scores to see "how you're doing". I'm not sure if he changed his perspective but I never forgot that moment and I enjoy pointing out this phenomenon to clients when I can.

4. Debt

A lot of clients come to my office absolutely, totally convinced they are the first people to ever face a lawsuit or a foreclosure. Ever. A perfectly understandable feeling. Being served papers tends to do that to the most rational of people.

Sometimes I point out that just a few blocks east from my office on Farmington Avenue is a pretty fabulous house – now a museum – that was also close to foreclosure back in the 1870's- the Mark Twain House. Mark Twain was a great author but a horrific businessman.

He faced foreclosure. Several times. He survived, is revered, and has awards named after him.

Debt is ageless, kind of like the oldest profession. Besides Twain, I have a few other examples of famous debt and foreclosures I pull out of my pocket when I think clients need a little perspective:

- Cinco de Mayo was really about a repossession
- The back story to *The DaVinci Code* was just about a guy who didn't want to pay his debt
- And Dickens' *A Christmas Carol* was a scathing response to those in the "top 1%"

§

Everyone loves Cinco de Mayo. What most people don't know is how the holiday came to be. It's not, as a lot of North-of-the-Border types believe, Mexican Independence Day. The 5th marks the Battle of Puebla in 1862 between French and Mexican forces in which a rag tag Mexican army of 2,000 routed a French army – that included a division of the Foreign Legion – of 8,000.

That's right, the French and Mexican armies fought a series of battles in the middle of our Civil War that eventually resulted in a French-installed government ruling Mexico until 1866.

Napoleon III's invasion and eventual takeover of Mexico was, in fact, perhaps the largest repossession action in history.

After the Mexican-American War and a series of revolutions and civil wars, Mexico was mired in debt and forced to suspend payments on its foreign debt. With the Civil War raging in the United States, Mexico's European creditors didn't have to worry about the Monroe Doctrine. The British and Spanish sent naval forces to Vera Cruz to register their displeasure, they quickly negotiated new repayment schedules. The French, however, were not so easily appeased (or maybe the new payment schedules with Spain and Britain left little for them) and so they invaded.

Cinco de Mayo was a successful debt defense worth celebrating. It should be noted, however, that while it was a spectacular upset, the victory was fleeting and Mexico was, in effect, in foreclosure for four very miserable years.

It was the military equivalent of firing off a strongly worded letter to a creditor, filing a complaint with the BBB, very satisfactorily slamming the phone down on the subsequent toll free call, only to watch the creditor exploit a rare loophole and still repossess your car.

Understanding what really went on gives me more reasons than tequila, great food and good company to celebrate Cinco de Mayo. It's somehow . . . empowering.

§

If you read Dan Brown's *The DaVinci Code* – or survived the movie – you may remember the hero, Robert Langdon, talking about the mysterious Knights Templar, driven underground by King Philip IV of France in the early 1300s.

They knew "great secrets" and were persecuted, hunted down, were believed to be wiped out but live on, unnoticed, influencing great events … you know the spiel.

Under Brown's layers of conspiracy theories is a historical truth that should speak loudly to millions of us today. The Templars did indeed very much exist. They were fabulously wealthy, the result of certain extracurricular activities during the Crusades.

They were entrenched in France when Philip ascended the throne. It being France and the Middle Ages, Philip spent most his time fighting the English. When peace broke out with them, he turned his attention to the Flemings.

Wars are, and have always been, expensive. Philip borrowed heavily from the Templars, probably far more than he or the kingdom could ever hope to repay.

He certainly could not maintain his wars or refill his empty coffers while repaying the Templars. For our purposes, think of being short of cash in the middle of February and needing to choose between paying the oil bill or CapitalOne.

Philip facing that same choice solved his fiscal quandary on Friday, October 13, 1307 by having the entire order of the Templars simultaneously arrested. End of the Templars, Philip burned his notes to them and…. well, the Templars as well. Then he confiscated all their holdings.

In one fell swoop Philip wiped out his debt and filled his coffers.

It's good to be king.

While most of us can only dream of taking care of our debt with such . . . finality . . . it's important to take a few lessons from this. First, debt, credit, debtors, creditors, collections, and defaults have been around for a very long time. Second, everyone – you, me, kings, queens, dictators, presidents, Founding Fathers – have debt. Lastly, we have options in how we handle that debt – not Philip's options – but options still, more than most people are aware they have.

§

Where would Charles Dickens have been without debt? Where would English Lit, Hollywood, and Christmas be without Dickens?

The running themes through Dickens' long – and lucrative – career were crushing debt, workhouses, courts snarled in technicalities, poverty, sour credit, low wages, foreclosures, banks, scams, mass incarceration, sweatshops, social injustice … All very much applicable today.

If Dickens came back tomorrow, he'd be astonished by the speed of today's communications; overwhelmed by the modern technologies used in finance; awed but probably pleased with the serialized novel on TV and Netflix, to just name a few– I imagine him binge watching *Breaking Bad* and *The Wire*.

He'd find some things appallingly the same, others miraculous. He'd immediately recognize Pharma Bro, everyone running for President, the characters in *The Big Short*. Give him a week and he'd be working on a new novel.

Dickens had an unfailing eye for all this because he lived it. He grew up in a middle-class family, comfortable, good at school, apparently fairly happy. All that was destroyed when he was twelve and his father was tossed into debtor's prison. Charles' mother and younger siblings went with him – as was the custom. Charles was forced to pawn his school books, was sent off to a workshop to help pay off his father's debts.

An inheritance saved the family though Dickens' mother was

adamantly opposed to his leaving work and forced him to stay there for long, unhappy months before he left to resume his studies. He rewarded her for that particular slight through dozens of novels and plays. (From Dickens to Bob Dylan and Alanis Morissette, it's never a good idea to upset an artist with wide reach.)

In his early writing career – he was pretty much a prodigy from the start – he covered the courts and, briefly, Parliament.

He saw the system from every angle and he set out to attack it in the only way he could, through his writing, within the flexibility and thin protection of the novel. He opened Victorian eyes to the seamy underbelly of British wealth, society, and empire.

In 1843 he turned his wrath to Christmas. At the time, many – including his good friend Washington Irving – felt that Christmas season was ebbing away from the poor and the increasingly put upon middle-class.

He didn't like what he was seeing and feeling, and he sat down to write a scathing pamphlet about the issue. It soon occurred to him that a novel would work much better, reach more people. In six weeks, he crafted his "ghost story," *A Christmas Carol.*

He published it himself in an effort to not be ripped off by his usual publisher. In today's parlance, it went viral. Immensely popular, even his (many) critics extolled it. Thousands and thousands of copies were sold, many more – particularly in the United States - were "bootlegged" and it was immediately adapted for the stage. Dickens himself did stage readings of the entire manuscript. It was everywhere.

Humanitarianism, redemption, a dead-on accurate portrayal of early-Victorian England, it hit a nerve in Great Britain and the United States. It hit, hard, the people bearing the burden of the Industrial Revolution, and changed the way everyone thought of the Christmas season.

How a man who, when first confronted with poverty and homelessness, says, "Are there no prisons? Are there no workhouses?" finds empathy is inspiring, regardless of religious belief. *A Christmas Carol* is a great story, a strong, bitter indictment of the times, and it worked. It changed things. It has never been out of print.

Again, no debt, no Dickens; no Dickens, no holiday season? The latter may be a stretch, but it's not unthinkable.

Every Christmas, I record the 1950 Alastair Sim, *A Christmas Carol* – a great adaptation (out of dozens, beginning with Thomas Edison's version in the early 1900s!).

I watch it during the holidays and think of my clients, with the obvious wish, "God bless us, everyone."

§

Who do you picture when you hear the word Foreclosure? Do you picture people sitting around piles of cash they have saved up because they haven't paid their mortgage? Do you picture people going on vacation on the money they saved by not paying their mortgage?

Do you think they are sleeping soundly on a bed of sweet-smelling flowers and wake up to rainbows?

Maybe that's what you picture, since we have been trained, as good Americans, to work hard and pay our bills. So if someone isn't paying their bills they must really be enjoying all the "extra" money they have hanging around. If we all believe that paying your bills = good and not paying bills = bad, then of course you think there is some benefit to the person not paying their bills, that they have "gotten away with something," and are getting rich in the process.

After years and years of working with people in debt, I can tell you not being able to pay bills comes with nothing but gray hair and sleepless nights.

I've been trying to figure out who is more likely to be in foreclosure so that I can "target" my advertising better. I want to focus my advertising time, energy and money on that group. The problem is, there is no ONE group more likely to be in foreclosure. I have helped doctors, lawyers, real estate agents, mortgage brokers, landscapers, painters, contractors, nurses, teachers, retirees, the disabled--you name it—who have all fallen on hard (or even harder) times. The only common denominator is owning a home. Whether your mortgage payment is $3000 per month or $900 per month, your home is your castle.

And hardship doesn't discriminate.

I have a list a mile long of the terrible things that happened to my clients before they fell behind on their bills, all which fall under the main categories of unemployment, divorce, disability or injury, having to care for someone sick, or death of a spouse or family member. That stuff can happen to anyone.

Believe me no one who isn't paying their mortgage is fat, happy and sitting on a pile of cash. They come to my office crying, depressed, sleep deprived and arguing with their spouse because of the stress that reduced household income and inability to pay bills causes. Don't think for a minute that the shame and embarrassment is any less for the house painter than the doctor, or that it's any easier for the real estate agent than the nurse to reach out for help.

I was talking to a real estate agent friend recently who just went through a major health crisis, which got worse while he was in denial about the seriousness of his condition before finally going to his doctor. His takeaway is that he feels we should all be talking about our issues and how they affect us and make us feel. He specifically said he's seeing a counselor to get over the stress he experienced while getting urgent medical treatment, and he thinks the more we all discuss that the better we will all be, and that we will be more likely to reach out for help when we need it sooner.

I couldn't agree more. I've been saying that for years, I even had the Got Debt? logo imprinted on my business cards for years because when I showed it to people it would make them smile and more likely to discuss money problems. In my experience, the sooner someone reaches out for help with their financial issues the more options they have. Nine times out of ten I'm told by clients speaking to me has helped them sleep much better immediately. At the very least, reaching out for help sooner can make you feel like you're sleeping on a bed of flowers.

5. Credit

I have theories about a lot of things, but here's a couple about credit for now.

First, I believe there is a connection between credit cards and wages.

Back in the early 1990s, the credit card interest rate rules started to change and lots more banks were offering lots more credit cards to lots more people. So much so that today the average person has something like 8 credit cards.

As De Niro says in *Casino* – "Just keep them playing."

Over the years, this changed our thinking to something I call "credit card mentality." Here's an example: I spoke with a man who was in a rage because his credit card company had lowered his available credit limit.

"They took my credit," was how he started the conversation. When I asked him to explain, he said he had a $10,000 limit, and a $4,000 outstanding balance he paid on every month. But then all of a sudden, the company lowered his credit limit to $4,000- so he had no more available credit. He felt robbed.

This is a widespread problem – Americans view their available credit as a savings account. We typically don't have much (or any) cash in savings accounts, but we can always charge it. To the point where it has become a point of pride to have a high credit line(s).

What does this have to do with wages? Well, another of my theories is that when people stopped worrying about having money in savings because they had plenty of available credit they stopped worrying about how much they were earning – they just charged when and where needed.

What happens then? No one demands higher wages, or if they do it's muted by the ready access to credit . . . it takes the bite out of the bark. Thus, the availability of credit has contributed to the stagnation of wages in the last generation, which as become a "credit card generation."

Is this sounding familiar at all? If you don't have 3-6 months of earnings saved in a savings account, then maybe this is why. If your earnings haven't kept up with your household expenses, maybe this is why. If you have credit card balances you can't seem to pay down, maybe this is why.

§

I have developed a few scripts working with people with debt and credit issues. I ask the same questions and say the same things over and over, because the situations I see are quite similar. Each person's facts and story is different, but the underlying themes and problems are alike. One of the questions I ask quite often is "When is the last time you saw your credit report?" Note that I don't say, "Have you seen your credit report?" or "What is your credit score?" I have carefully crafted this question after many drafts in order to get the answer I am looking for, which is exactly when is the last time the person I am talking to saw their credit report.

The most common answer, I can practically lip sync it, is, "I don't want to see my credit!"

A close second is, "I'm afraid to look."

My response, based on having looked at as many credit reports as a medical intern has taken blood pressure readings, goes like this: "Well, everyone else is looking at it, you should too. And besides, it's never as bad as you think it is going to be." Both points are true.

I love giving people good news, especially when a negative myth, a total misunderstanding, or inaccurate assumption has controlled their experience with their credit.

For example, I will sometimes ask, before asking about the last time they checked their credit report, what they think they are going to see. Why are they calling me—what do they think they need to correct? (It is amazing how many people call the office, leading with, "I want to fix my credit," but they have not seen a copy of their credit report in years, if ever.)

One woman told me she was worried about her Sears account.

"Why?" I asked.

"Well," she replied, "when my husband and I got married, we bought a refrigerator from Sears and we put it on credit. But then my husband lost his job and we couldn't pay for it anymore, and I'm worried it's hurting my credit."

"When did you get married?" I ask, expecting something like two or three years ago.

"We've been married seventeen years," she answered. She did not know that the statute of limitation on an unpaid account had likely long run out and an unpaid item will only appear on her credit for at most about 7 years, so this Sears card was not likely to still be marring her credit.

I think this anecdote speaks as much to what things the average person feels are important—to her, not repaying Sears caused her guilt; she had no other more recent credit issues that she felt bad about that she could recall.

Talk about being able to deliver good news. I met with a couple in their early thirties a few years back. They were referred to me by a mortgage broker because they wanted to buy a home. I scheduled an appointment to review their credit since they were convinced they were going to have to file for bankruptcy. Or so they said as I led them into my conference room.

About a minute after sitting down and reviewing their credit reports, I knew why they were concerned: I saw about $42,000 in unpaid, overdue accounts, including a couple of small claims judgments from a neighboring state.

I know what to look for and showed them that about $30,000 of the debt was so old that it was going to "age off" their credit within a few months, and another several thousand within 6 months.

They were amazed. They had lived for months, probably a few years, believing they had to pay off *all* this debt, letting it weigh them down.

In my state, an unpaid account goes stale after 6 years. That is, if the company they owed tries to sue them more than 6 years from the last payment, the company cannot collect because they sued beyond the statute of limitations.

This was the case with most of their debt, except the judgments. We just had to track down the lawyers who had brought those suits and relay a settlement offer. Once we did that, the clients were able to settle the judgments and the small remaining accounts for a total of about $4,500. That was fun.

§

What is your comfort level with credit card debt? How much do you have, if any? The typical response to "How much credit card debt do you have?" is usually to underestimate the total by several thousand dollars. That's ok. I ask people I meet with to bring in a list of their current outstanding balances. One gentleman was a woodworker and he brought his list in scrawled on a piece of 2" x 6" pine!

Before scheduling an appointment with someone to discuss their credit card debt, I usually determine whether the person is a good candidate for filing bankruptcy. It is not my goal to charge someone money to listen to my advice if what they should really do is just go file for bankruptcy.

But if someone doesn't quite have enough debt, or if they have a major objection to filing for bankruptcy, or if they have an asset that prevents them from qualifying for a no-asset Chapter 7 bankruptcy, I offer a sane alternative. After screening out those who should just file bankruptcy, the people I do meet with believe that the only alternative is to pay, and that is tough because they usually don't have the income or cash flow to keep up even the minimum payments on their accounts.

I routinely meet with people whose credit card debt exceeds $20,000. It's not unusual for someone to come in with upwards of $95,000 of credit card debt. There are at least three notable situations where I helped people through that nightmare from beginning to end.

§

The Goldmans were perhaps the first couple I met who had over $90,000 in outstanding balances. They came to me early on in my practice of counseling people through this kind of crisis. Their situation was otherwise typical: loss of employment had caused them to incur additional charges. One spouse had to live and work out of state, which caused additional housing and travel expenses.

They had quite a bit of equity in their house—too much, even after the real estate market crash of 2008, to fall within the low asset limits to file for bankruptcy—but they could not tap into it because their income had been reduced and their credit had taken a hit. When they came to see me they were stressed over the debt and their respective anxieties about it were palpable.

It would not have surprised me if they had contemplated divorce but couldn't afford to do it! My advice: stop paying the cards. Stop now, they couldn't afford any minimums anymore.

When you stop paying, commit to that plan. Stop for three months, and then the accounts will go into collection. Here's how to handle all the calls you will get. Here's what to do with the bills. If you can live with that plan, you will soon come out of the woods.

How is this possible? That, of course, is the question everyone asks when I give them this advice. Everyone imagines that an unpaid or a late bill is a direct route to the sky falling. It isn't. Here's what will happen: you will get calls, you will get letters, and eventually you may be sued. That's it.

That's it?

Yes, unless you stop paying on your car, your house, or some other "secured" asset or object, where the lender has a lien on the item. That's it: you will get calls, you will get letters, and eventually you may be sued.

But....

There are always a few buts: Can't they (they being Discover, Chase, American Express, Bank of America, etc.) take my wages? Won't they take money out of my bank account? Won't they... repossess my car? Tell my boss? Call my mother? Cancel my other accounts? Tell the IRS? Tell the judge? Interrogate me? Make me pay it all at once? Have me arrested?

I calmly address these questions, which are all valid. Not only do they make sense; they are an indication that this person was raised to work hard and pay their bills, and just can't imagine a world in which they can't pay their bills. Therefore, it's not surprising that they have created a doomsday scenario in which the sky falls and the boogeyman comes out of the closet the minute they are late on a bill.

They are amazed that this never happens. Some are even disappointed. It's as if they would prefer to be punished in exchange for not paying their bills; that, for some reason, would make sense. Being able to just stop paying and not suffer doesn't make sense.

I gave the Goldmans this advice. They came in telling me they could no longer handle paying all their credit card minimums, so I gave them license to do what they could no longer do anyways, stop paying. They left with my instructions on how to handle what would come next, with an invitation to keep in touch throughout the following months.

I'm sure they checked in over the next few weeks, but I specifically remember a phone call I received from Mrs. Goldman about two months after they stopped paying. She asked me whether she should pick up the calls; one creditor had been calling them consistently and she wondered if she should explain why they hadn't been paying.

I advised her not to waste her time, that everyone who was

behind on payments had a similar story—loss of employment, illness, etc., that prevented them from being able to pay. But what she really meant was, "Won't they bring this up later in court, that we never answered their calls? Won't that be held against us?"

It was a brilliant question. In all the months and years I have been counseling people around their credit card debt, I continue to learn more about the psychology of being in debt. It's revealed in questions like this: Mrs. Goldman thought the system was so personalized that a big company would be personally offended that she didn't answer their calls, and the failure to communicate with them would be a factor if the account were ever taken to court.

This has probably gone through the mind of many a client of mine but because the answer is "No, this will not matter later," my counseling never addressed it. Now I always bring this up and it is always part of my regular advice.

I think the Goldmans came to see me in 2010. Over the next few years they got calls and letters. I ask clients to keep track of all of that; you never know when the calls are going to pile up to the level where it constitutes harassment. At least two debt collectors crossed the line when contacting the Goldmans and engaged in abusive conduct. I sued those collectors. We settled those matters, and interestingly, and this became a pattern, the settlements occurred just around the time my clients were brought to court on another account.

They needed representation in that collection case, so I arranged for them to let me use a portion of the harassment case settlement money as retainer to represent them in the collection case. Note that this way the clients did not have to write me a check- their fees were covered, for the most part, by settlements with the debt collectors who had harassed them.

I represented the Goldmans in a few court cases, some small claims and some larger court cases. Out of the $95,000 of credit card debt they started with, a surprisingly small amount of that debt was ever brought to court. In their case, it was less than a third of their total. A typical settlement with a creditor, in my experience, is about 50-60% of the total amount claimed.

In the five years after the Goldmans stopped paying their credit cards we were able to take $95,000 and reduce it to about $30,000 in litigated debt, of which they had to pay about $18,000 total. Not bad.

§

Paula is a well-paid nurse whose income was strained by paying a mortgage while having to send money to support her family back in her home country. She also had to travel back to her home country at least once per year.

When she came to see me, she was struggling to maintain her credit card minimum payments on $95,000 in total debt. I gave her the same advice- stop paying. The good thing about Paula was she could work extra shifts doing home health care and could squirrel that money away in anticipation of settling her accounts.

Over several years she was sued to collect on her balances, but the lawsuits were spread out. My experience is that people who stop paying their accounts do not get sued all at once (of course this can occur and I have had clients who have had bad luck with this), but for the most part, suits are usually spread out over months or years. This isn't intentional, it just seems to happen that way.

Some cases to collect are harder to win or settle than others. Discover and American Express and other "original creditors"- that is, the companies that actually loaned the funds- can usually prove their cases without much trouble. Compare this to the "debt buyer" who purchased an unpaid account and has little or no evidence of the purchase, proof that it bought the account, or how the card was used.

One of the largest suits brought against Paula was brought by a debt buyer who purchased one of her unpaid accounts. Although this kind of case should be easy to beat, all but the most activist judges seem to "rubber stamp" judgments against consumers for unpaid credit card debt. Here, though, not only was the proof very slim, but the attorney who brought the case had engaged in some actions that could constitute harassment under the law.

We asserted those claims and the collection case ended up being dropped. Paula is not out of the woods on her $95,000 debt; there is still one unpaid account and she is still saving up to be able to settle it. But over the years she has only had to pay a fraction of each of the claims brought against her.

§

James also came to me almost six figures in debt. He brought a spreadsheet itemizing his accounts, the current balances, the date he last paid, and the interest rates. He was being sued for the account with the largest balance, a home equity line taken on an investment property he owned in another state that he lost to foreclosure during the crash in 2008.

It was a relatively large balance bought from the original lender by a debt buyer. We asked the debt buyer for information from the original account as James believed he had made more payments than claimed. The documentation provided us was confusing at best, and appeared to be filled with inaccuracies. We went to trial and the witness from the debt buyer did not, I felt, interpret the documents from the original creditor sufficiently. But even with what I took to be glaring inconsistencies in the documentation of the alleged debt, and the debt buyer's inability to prove their case, they won. Sigh.

The only way I can stay sane in situations like that is to recall the words of wisdom of the attorney who hired me out of law school: "Judges tend to make up their minds about a case and then find a way to get there".

In the end, the creditor accepted a payment from James that was about 50-60% of their claim. Even though they had a judgment, he was still able to get a discount. It wasn't ideal, but sometimes having a judgment resolved is more valuable than living with a debt hanging over your head.

You may be somewhat appalled or disgusted that these people were able to "charge up" their balances and then "get away with" only paying a very small portion of their debts. To those of us who are paying our debts dollar-for-dollar, it does sound a bit unfair.

But here's an important lesson: if the Goldmans, and Paula, and James each had to pay off $95,000 of debt, what does that do to their ability to pay their mortgages, pay for medical care, and save for retirement?

Believe me, no one goes into the plan of not paying their cards lightly or willingly. There is a lot of resistance to following my strategy. When someone says, I want to pay ALL my debt, or when they raise a religious or moral objection, I point this out: if they only earn $50,000 per year, how many years will it take to pay down $95,000 of credit card debt?

Forever. Their entire working lives.

My system "stops the bleeding," that is, it draws a line in the sand and starts the clock ticking on the statute of limitations on repayment of debt. If a creditor blows the deadline, that is the creditor's choice. In the meantime, hard-earned money isn't flowing to the over-paid CEOs of the credit card companies, it is staying in the pockets of the hard-working client. And going into their retirement funds.

When someone scoffs at the idea of not their paying bills, even if they can't afford to make the payments, I look them in the eye and say, "It is not in society's interest for you to be a poor, old woman." What

I mean is, Social Security is only going to pay for so much, and it's not much. We each need to be building up our retirement accounts. If the next $95,000 earned by Paula or James or the Goldmans goes to creditors, they aren't saving for retirement. This helps no one.

The CEOs won't miss my clients' $50 per month minimum payments; but for each of us, that's all we have, our ability to put $50 a week or month – more or less- away for retirement. This plan, then, is good for my clients, *and* for you and me.

6. Middle Class

The middle class is an interesting place to be. You can go your whole life and pretty much never meet anybody who is not in the middle class. It's a very low risk place to live. So low-risk most of us are not taught how to think big. Even though we really have no idea what that means.

So, we dream of winning the lottery.

Maybe someone will win $10,000 on a scratch ticket occasionally, or take a chance at the roulette wheel and net a five-figure return, but none of that pulls you out of the middle class. That's just a windfall. That's just the one bonus you might ever see in your life.

Being middle-class means you think a tax refund is a big deal. Being middle-class means you don't understand that the tax refund was your money you loaned to the government for 12 months and then had to ask to get it back.

The plight of the middle class is that we think small. We can't bear to think big. Nothing trains us to think big. There's no insurance if thinking big doesn't work. We think there's nothing to fall back on if we flop. Sure, we learn in school about the outlier inventors and risk takers and military leaders who made an actual impact on the world, but no one ever tells us how we could be them. No one ever *REALLY* tells us how we could be them. Because the people teaching us have no idea how to be them.

Very few of us grew up with an entrepreneur to mentor us, someone who really takes risks. The closest thing any of us ever got to that is probably the older kid on the block you grew up on who dared to ride his bike without holding onto the handlebars, or who would jump off that tall wall or take that high dive at the local swimming hole.

That kid was trying to think big. That kid had a shot out of the middle class. But no one recognized it as such. Those risks were seen as reckless and were discouraged, punished and certainly not seen as the urgent desire to be something bigger and grander than middle class.

That kid would've had to be plucked out of that swimming hole or off that high dive by someone who had already taken risks and seen beyond the limits of the middle class, to become anything but middle-class. To become anything but eventually an irreverent 40-year-old, whose best days were those junior high and high school days when he was free to ride his bike without holding the handlebars.

There have been a few people who have emerged from the middle class but they scare the rest of us in the middle class. They've gotten out of the middle class by selling something, which is seen as something dirty to the middle class. Being salesy is a problem for us average middle-class people. We're trained to not be pushy, to be polite and nice. We're supposed to be kind and generous and do unto others. So, your fellow middle-class citizens discourage you from doing the things that you need to do to get out of the middle class.

It's risky to sell. You risk not being liked. But no one ever got a different result by doing the same thing over and over. That is a symptom of someone who is in the middle class. Get up, go to work, come home, watch TV, go to bed, get up, go to work, come home, watch TV, go to bed…

Sometimes we have the chance to be great, or feel like we are great. Those are called our one-week vacations. Where we emerge from our routines and do something different for a few days. Maybe spend a little too much money, swipe those credit cards and feel rich for a few days. Treat ourselves to an extra glass of wine or tell the kids, "Sure you can have whatever you want."

Then vacation is over. And we go back to our routines. Where we take no risks, where we do things over and over the same way. I know it's a cliché by now but they say if you continue to do the same thing over and over and expect different results it is the definition of insanity.

Talk to anyone in the middle class and they will tell you that their big break, their big winning lottery ticket is right around the corner. It's that next scratch ticket that you spend the extra dollar to buy just in case. It's the office pool that buys 100 Powerball tickets. Somehow that dream is enough for someone in the middle class. Somehow it can keep you going for years.

§

It's completely unfair. We exchange the chance for real excitement, for real adventure, for exhilarating fear, a true chance at greatness, for the safety of the middle class. Our Stone Age human survival and safety instincts keep us there. We exchange the chance at greatness for a lifetime of predictability and stability. Or at least an expectation of predictability and stability.

"I have a home to go home to, I have food in my refrigerator, a car in the garage and a job to go to."

"I have my direct deposit, that I know will be there every other Thursday."

"I know what to expect every day."

There is value to those sentiments. I can't say I don't enjoy my basic middle-class comforts. I can't say I wouldn't be afraid if given the chance to emerge from the middle class I had to leave all its comforts behind, at least temporarily. I, too, fear the unknown and prefer to stay in the known versus taking chances. Therefore, I am middle class. And here I remain.

I work with very interesting people. They are all middle-class. The middle class has a very broad range, from people who think living in a house worth $100,000 is a castle to people who are embarrassed by their million-dollar home because it's not a $2 million home. They all have one thing in common though. Hardship is hardship. And when it hits someone at the lower end of the income spectrum or hits someone at the higher end the results seem to be the same.

Hardship is a very difficult thing to emerge from, just like emerging from the middle class is almost impossible. Hardship changes your mindset. You don't exactly lose hope, you just reduce your expectations and change your tolerances. You reduce your expectations of yourself, and really tap into how exhausting it is being middle class. When you are tossed out of your middle-class routine by something like job loss or illness, you really start to feel the fatigue.

I'm amazed at how exhausted and depressed people who aren't working are. They are drained of all energy, they are drained of all direction. Whether they were millionaire financial guys or barely in the middle-class landscapers, if they lose work, they become the same person.

They don't take a loss of work as an opportunity to leap into the unknown., they don't see it as their chance to be who they wanted to be when they used to ride down the street on their bikes without holding onto the handlebars. They don't do anything that scares them.

On the contrary, loss of the routine and a regular income just forces them to see how little they can live on. Now it's almost a challenge to stay in the middle class, to stay as average as possible, as average as you were before you lost your job.

You may have hated your job before, but now all you can dream of is applying for the same job you had before, because at least you knew what to expect. At least it was the known. And when that same old job with that same old income doesn't come around in a year or two, even the job at the local coffee shop seems to look good.

It's discouraging how our middle-class upbringing does not prepare us for the opportunity that a big change in life can present. Sure, it's risky, sure you risk losing out on obtaining that same old job and that same old paycheck if you look in a completely different direction and take a leap into the unknown.

If you start to really dream big and think, "Here's my chance finally to start living my dream," you risk missing that opportunity to go back to your old life. We are not outfitted with the skills it takes to emerge from the middle class and the middle-class mindset. We don't even have the skills to go from lower middle-class to middle class. Or from middle middle-class to upper-middle-class.

That's why it sucks to be middle-class. You can work for 40 years waiting to retire, but there's still no guarantee that you will have the means to live the way you want to when you retire. Somehow that is socially acceptable in our middle-class society. It's acceptable for someone to go through a lifetime of thinking middle class and maybe preparing as best as possible for those dream days of retirement, but to still not have enough to live the way you want to when you retire. Somehow that's OK with the rest of us. Somehow the person who worked their whole life and did not manage to save enough to be able to go golfing all day as a retiree caused that problem themselves. This is an interesting corollary to the middle class' inability to dream big.

First, we think that being able to go golfing every day when you retire is a big dream. But second, we criticize those who are unable to do that when they retire. The irony is going golfing every day in retirement is so far off from the routine that you had when you were living your middle-class working life and yet we criticize each other for not easily converting our lives from the work all day go home go to bed get up go to work all day go home go to bed routine, into the routine of a retiree.

We criticize those who have not set themselves up during their working life (who have not ever changed their routine or obtained the skills necessary to get out of the middle class) to be able to emerge from that middle-class routine when they retire. Maybe that's our Stone Age instincts searching for safety and security that come out in response to seeing someone else not live their dream. Why we think our retirement will be any different is beyond me. We sit here in our glass houses with a handful of stones.

It really stinks to be middle-class. Correction, it stinks to be middle-class and to want more, and to not have the courage to get out of the middle class. It reminds me of this - I have an aunt who has Down Syndrome. When I was a kid, I asked my mother, who is her oldest sister, "Do you think Mary knows she has a handicap?" I don't remember what my mother said, but I think it was something along the lines of "Sometimes you're better off not knowing or not understanding."

If you're in the middle class and you don't really care about being anything but middle-class, and you never really think about how you are stuck in a routine and how you are never taught how to get out of that routine, or that you're surrounded by people who do not want you to get out of that routine, your life will be just fine.

But it stinks to be in the middle class and know you're in the middle class and know that there could be a way out but that you just don't have it in you to get out. I really believe that we all could get out, if only we understood what it really takes to get out, what getting out means, and were willing to do what it takes to get out. My idea of an opportunity to get out is when your safety and your security is taken away from you. But unfortunately, something drives us to cling to the vestiges of what we knew of the old safety and security we had even when that is taken away from us, and not try to create a new type of safety and security for ourselves, that could be bigger and better than what we had when we were middle-class.

Being the kid who took the high dives at the local swimming hole was hard. There wasn't enough of that type around in any one place, at any one time to make that type of risk OK. If only we could turn our middle-class "Ride your bike to work" days into "Ride your bike to work without holding the handle bars" days, then maybe we would have a shot at breaking out of this middle class.

§

Speaking of the middle-class, virtually everyone in it has a thirty-year mortgage. Almost no one thinks about the implications of thirty years. Most people are so happy to qualify for a mortgage and buy a home they're only focused on the rate and the monthly payment.

Consumers, especially those flushed with the excitement of buying their first home, tend to overlook a cold, hard fact: *Thirty years is a long time.* Few, if anything, lasts thirty years. Not even the Thirty Years War really lasted thirty years. Not continuously, at least.

It's not all that easy to think back thirty years. Ferris Bueller's day off was thirty years ago. There are a great many diehard baseball fans that couldn't tell you that the Kansas City Royals defeated the Cardinals in the 1985 World Series. Especially since the Royals promptly disappeared from view until 2015.

In the last thirty years we've had six Presidents; been in three wars; through three 'official' recessions, eight stock market crashes; countless bull and bear markets; seen cell phones go from the Gordon Gekko size of a small briefcase to smart phones; seen technological advances that were only foreseen by science fiction.

Thirty Years. That's the average life span of a Fortune 500 company. Actually, absent Coca Cola and a few others, almost two-thirds of the Fortune 500 list turns over every thirty years or so (who remembers Compaq computers?).

The average marriage in the United States lasts roughly 14 years. Regardless, more than 60% of marriages end in 21 or so years by divorce or death of a spouse. The average worker changes jobs about every five years.

Thirty years of perfect health – physical and mental -would be an outlier of epic proportions.

And yet thirty years is overwhelmingly the term for most mortgages in the U.S.

When I meet with a new client it's important that they know what this means. That no one can control – maybe even influence all that much – events over a 30-year span. Certainly not their health, career, market forces, recessions, corporate mergers /bankruptcies/ relocations/relevance; marriage; children; aging/ailing parents; severe weather; and a hundred other things.

Thirty years is a long time to pay for a house, a lot can and will happen, a lot of it is not within anyone's control.

§

The last part of that last sentence is something I constantly have to remind clients of: *A lot of it is not within anyone's control.* It's a hard thing to accept, no one wants to think of things beyond their control – they want to leave all that to hurricanes and blizzards.

A little while back the *New York Times* ran an article called The Psychology of Choking Under Pressure. I'm not a big proponent of the term "choking" but I understand why they used it in this article.

It's really about how people sense the "stakes" they are working/playing for.

The study the *Times* quotes reveals some pretty counter-intuitive findings (and sounds a lot like a paraphrase of my thoughts on the Middle Class above):

It may be that those of us who don't like losses also have an exaggerated fear of failure, so we regard that opportunity to win $100 not as a chance for gain but as an outsize opportunity to fail. Conversely, people more comfortable with loss might harbor a surprising intolerance for losing what they already have.

This is interesting stuff and I encourage you to check out the article. Being who I am and what I do, when I read it I thought, "How does this manifest in my clients who are in debt or who are in foreclosure?"

I see the fear of opportunity from many of my clients – it usually looks like anger, utter desolation, out-of-body optimism, doom and gloom; outright resignation, and a lot more. A good, good chunk of my early work with a new client is explaining that *it's not over*. There are options; you just need to make a new decision, you aren't on an irreversible course to losing your house; even if you are, there are paths to ease or minimize the impact.

When I was trying to decide where to take my first job out of law school, I turned to a classmate who had already had a career in corporate America and went to law school as a second act. He said, "If this is not the right decision, then you make another decision. Not every decision is a win." At the time I made the right decision. Then I made a new one.

When meeting with a new client, I try to define, up front, what a "win" would be in any given foreclosure case. As the article says, ". . . *For now, the practical takeaway seems to be that you should figure out your tolerance for loss and frame high-pressure situations accordingly. You are likely to find it easier to avoid choking if you take into account your complicated relationship to winning.*"

A complicated relationship with winning. I get that. I also get that telling a client that they can "win" their foreclosure sounds strange, but given the options that doesn't make it any less true.

7. Lessons

I was lucky to have parents with good financial management skills who imparted some very important nuggets on the importance of being organized with your money.

I have a sister 14 months older than me. We would often do our homework at the kitchen table. So would my mother. What do I mean by that? I mean she did her "adult homework" alongside us. About twice a month she'd join us after dinner with the check book and the pile of household bills. She wasn't thrilled about this task, I specifically remember a lot of audible sighing during the process. But she methodically organized the bills, detached the payment stubs from the rest of the statement, wrote out the check, filled in the amount paid on the payment coupon, filled in the check number, date, payee and amount in the check register, placed the check and payment coupon in the envelope, sealed it, stamped it and wrote in the return address. Bill after bill we would watch her do this while we did our math or science homework. Month after month, year after year. When it was my time to have a check book and monthly bills, I knew just what to do, including exactly when to let out a loud sigh.

§

I believe it's the luck of the draw when you have a parent who is financially organized (not necessarily rich, just organized), and understands how the system works. I picked up, from watching my mother pay the household bills, that there are due dates on bills and they need to be paid on time. There was an "or else" implied there, and the more I work with people in financial distress I realize everyone has their own idea of what "or else" means. In the "Lessons From Mom" context, I believed it meant, "Or else you won't have the ability to be able to buy the things you want," in addition to the implication that bad things might happen if you paid bills late or skipped payments.

Mom wanted us to understand this, as well as that we should be able to have and use credit cards. When we started driving, she added our names to her gas credit card accounts. We were issued cards in our names with her account number. Her instructions were to use it to buy one tank of gas per month on the card, and then we or she would pay it off. She wanted us to be able to "piggy back" on her good credit rating.

The other advice she gave I still discuss to this day when I talk about building credit. My mother said to us, "When you turn 18, go to Filene's, buy yourself a bra, and when they ask you if you'd

94

like to apply for the store credit card, say yes. Charge the bra on the card, and pay it off. Then when you need underwear, use the card, and pay it off."

The point was to use credit sparingly and responsibly early on to build credit so that we'd have access to more credit later when needed. The other implied message, which is equally important, was to use someone else's money for your benefit, and to do that you should follow the rules by using it sparingly and paying it off quickly. Credit is a tool that can help you if used correctly but can hurt you if you don't.

§

In 2005, I went to a consumer law conference and bought a book called *"The Two-Income Trap: Why Middle-Class Mothers and Fathers are Going Broke,"* and I became an immediate fan. The authors are former law professor, now Senator from Massachusetts, Elizabeth Warren and her daughter Amelia Tyagi-Warren. Their goal was to explain to the world, including those broke, middle-class parents, how people get into financial trouble.

I talk about this book all the time and every day I filter my clients' experiences through the concepts Warren covers in the book. I recall purchasing the book using the law firm credit card of the small consumer law practice I worked in at the time. When I informed my boss that I had used the firm card to buy it, he, at the time, asked me to reimburse the firm as he didn't see how the book was something of interest to the firm.

A year later, Warren was the keynote speaker at the next big annual consumer law conference that my boss attended and he came back raving about her. I felt like I was ahead of the curve by my early appreciation of her relevance to our work.

Then I discovered another Warren book titled *All Your Worth…* I just can't get enough of her writing.

A brief summary of some of Elizabeth Warren's awesome clarity on the topic of debt and the average American:

Don't borrow to get out of debt.

I have passed this concept on to many a conscientious consumer. I only get so many phone calls; that is, people who call me generally have issues that fall into one of about four main topics. One call I often get is the person who has too much credit card debt and wants to consolidate their account balances. People think this is a solution to having too much debt but it doesn't change the amount of debt.

Consolidating debt means you borrow a large sum of money to pay off lots of smaller sums of money and you end up with one big loan payment instead of multiple accounts with smaller balances. This appeals because now you only have one monthly payment instead of having to keep track of multiple payment amounts and multiple payment deadlines; and you feel like you have taken a step toward paying off your (usually very high) debt because now you only have one loan.

I can appreciate the desire to "do the right thing" and pay off your many accounts in one fell swoop, but this is simply borrowing to get out of debt and it's not a good idea. It doesn't really change your situation.

I believe the person who wants to take out a consolidation loan is only doing it because they don't know what else to do. They believe they *should* <u>do</u> something, and they want to do the *right* thing.

They have no intention of ever skipping a payment which is perceived as a terrible thing. The messages in the media (at least according to the ads on commercial rock-and-roll radio stations during rush hour and the ads that run on cable television late at night) are that you must avoid bankruptcy, that bankruptcy is a terrible thing and people who file for bankruptcy are terrible people. None of that is true and the ads steer you away from bankruptcy and toward borrowing to get out of debt as if that is the only option.

I advise my clients not to borrow to get out of debt because they either should just go speak to a bankruptcy attorney and explore that option, or they should just stop paying their credit card debt altogether. Warren can't go deep into this kind of advice; that is, she can discuss the option of filing for bankruptcy and encourage readers to evaluate and prioritize what bills to pay and when, but she can't give advice that is so specific it becomes legal advice. I have the luxury, however, of being able to do that with residents of my state where I am licensed to practice law.

Someone will call me and say they are considering a debt consolidation loan. I'll speak to them for a few minutes and ask why they are interested in that option and it's always the same two reasons: they think it's the right thing to do because they can't keep up with all their various accounts, and they don't think they have any other options under the circumstances.

After a brief discussion, I refer about half the people who call me with this issue to a bankruptcy attorney and they usually end up filing. The other half either can't file for bankruptcy because they are disqualified for some reason (too much income, too many assets, or have filed in the too recent past), and I offer them a consultation in my office. Here is where I end up blowing their minds.

The client comes in with a list of their outstanding credit card debts. I ask them to prepare this list before our meeting and I routinely meet with people with 7, 8, 9, 10 or more credit cards and typically between $40,000 and $95,000 in outstanding balances.

I discuss elsewhere in this book that these are not frivolous people who just lost track of their spending while on vacation one time. These are the typical middle-class mothers and fathers like those described in *The Two-Income Trap* who have suffered a hardship, generally two or more hardships in a short period (divorce and illness of a child; unemployment of one spouse and injury to the other; property damage due to storms and an injury that kept one spouse out of work; there are endless combinations).

Warren points out that the typical middle-class family hit by hardship does not immediately uproot themselves and their children from their suburban home and move to a more affordable rental unit in a different, less desirable school district.

The typical family just uses their available credit limits to bridge the income gap. Then before they know it one month turns into three, then into six months of trouble, and by the time a job is found, it is probably not the same income as the last job so the family now also has to struggle with the hangover of their hardship- large credit card balances: "legacy debt." I can't remember where I heard the term—it's probably Warren's – but it perfectly describes these high balances left over from that period of hardship. That is what most people who file for bankruptcy or who come to me for advice have—a large amount of "legacy debt."

The advice I give that blows people away is "Just stop paying." Their inevitable response is, "What? I can't do that!" Without advice and guidance, you shouldn't do that. In fact, get a legal opinion first. Have a discussion with an attorney who understands the consequences of not paying credit card debt and can advise accordingly, based on your own individual facts.

How is not paying better than a consolidation loan? First, a consolidation loan (or doing a credit card balance transfer) is essentially taking a cash loan from one source to pay off multiple account balances.

The problems start if you can't make the payment on that new consolidation loan. Before the loan, you had several accounts with smaller balances and your payment due dates were likely staggered throughout the month. After the loan, you have one payment that is going to be roughly equal to the sum of all your smaller payments and it is going to be due by a certain date each month.

Let's say before the loan you have 5 cards with balances totaling $8500 with minimum monthly payments due of $50, $100, $125, $75 and $60. All are due at different times of the month so you get to spread the $410 in minimums over the entire month, usually paying one or two bills out of each paycheck. Let's say the payment on your consolidation loan is $375 but due the 15th of the month. You have to go from spreading out the smaller payments over several weeks to finding $375 smack dab in the middle of the month, no matter when you get paid.

If you fall behind on *THIS* payment, then you owe one company $8500 and that company may sue you for payment. Before the loan you had balances of something like $1500, $2500, $1250, $2000 and $1200. Each of those balances separately would fall into the Small Claims court in my state, but $8500 would not.

Typically, if you stop paying credit cards, not only does it usually take at least six months or more for the company you owe to sue you for payment, but the companies usually do not all sue you at once.

You may find yourself defending a $1500 small claim suit one year, a $2500 suit nine months later, etc. The benefit to that (if it can be considered a benefit), is that you can probably save up enough to make a settlement on the $1500 account and get the case dropped, and then save up again in anticipation of another case being filed against you.

If you fall behind on an $8500 consolidation loan balance, you would have to save up a lot more to settle that one. If you can't settle, you will likely end up with an $8500 judgment against you (instead of, say, a $1500 judgment). It just changes everything.

So don't borrow to get out of debt. Because…

. . .Debt Steals From Your Future.

This is the next of Warren's lessons. When you have debt you are "in the red," you are in a negative situation. When you have debt you are essentially only working to pay off yesterday's cheeseburgers (to misquote Popeye's friend Wimpy). That steals from your future because you are scrambling to make up for past spending. You can see how in this context, borrowing to get out of debt does not help you get out of a negative situation.

The goal is to get out of debt as soon as possible so you can move forward, so the dollars you earn today can pay for things you need today, and not compete with the things you bought yesterday.

I can appreciate all the people who want to pay off every penny of their debt. I worked with a woman who was being sued for $12,000. Somehow we managed to get the creditor to settle for $2,500. As my client was agreeing to pay that, she told me she wished she could pay the whole thing.

I know she meant, "I wish I had never fallen behind and could have just made all the payments." But years on, hardship still dogging her, she truly wanted to pay more. There is a moral element to paying off debt that I can appreciate but she would be so much further behind financially today had she been on the hook for the whole amount. At least I know that she bought herself some of her future back by settling and paying less.

§

I was asked to speak on a panel at a conference for young women. The moderator asked us if we had just a few words of advice to share with the high school and college-aged attendees, what would that advice be? I wasn't expecting the question but by the time it was my turn, I realized my advice to women—to anyone really—is "Do the Math."

In law school I took a class on Federal Taxation the first semester of my second year. I wasn't at all interested in Federal Taxation (you know, learning about income taxes and the other IRS laws), but I needed the credits and it was a 4-credit class in a sea of 3-credit options.

Surprisingly, I was hooked after the first class. There were probably 40 students and I could tell the professor was going to be one of the smartest people I had ever met. He spent most of the first class session introducing us to the outline of the class and he even had a few tricks up his sleeve to show us how fun Federal Taxation could be.

First, he unfolded a large piece of paper—I mean bigger than that Farah Fawcett poster that most guys had hanging in their bedrooms as teenagers in the 70s—and hung it up over the chalkboard. It was a huge version of the 1040 tax form.

Somehow seeing the form enlarged to a ridiculous proportion made the idea of filing a tax return so much less intimidating. Then he proceeded to share some tricks and tips about filing taxes—such as if you mail in a check to pay taxes you owe, put the check in a microwave oven for just a couple of seconds before sealing it up and sending it off; the microwave messes with the magnetic codes or numbers or whatever is embedded in checks so that the IRS's machines couldn't read it and the check would have to be processed manually, thus leaving your money in your account for a few extra days. I really respected a professor who knew how to take a dry, intimidating subject like the IRS code and make it seem cool.

In the last few minutes of that first class, after he had dispelled the myths of the big, bad IRS, he asked, "Any questions?"

In the front row on the opposite side of the room from me sat a fellow female 2nd year student. While most of us were obviously engaged and ready for more, she had slipped down in her chair. She shyly raised her hand and what came out of her mouth indicated to me that she and I had been listening to a completely different presentation for the previous hour and a half: "Is there going to be a lot of math involved?" she squeaked.

I cringed. I wanted to scream at her. I was not a big fan of math but there was no indication in the summary the professor gave that we were going to be required to do any specific calculations. I didn't so much want to scream at her as curse the society that convinces girls and women that they can't do math, that it's hard and that it's scary.

To her credit, she was probably only 22 or 23 and I was about to turn 30, so I had lived in the real world a little longer, I had had to manage a household budget, balance a checkbook and file my own tax returns for several years before going to law school. I still wasn't a big fan of anything more than household math basics but I felt like this professor would be holding our hand if we had to do any kind of calculations.

My fellow student disappointed me in that she bought into the idea that math was hard. Here was someone who got into law school, made it through a grueling first year, and *STILL* felt she needed some notice of having to deal with math problems.

By the way, one-third of the law school entrance exam includes "games," complex and seemingly illogical word problems that require the test-taker to sketch out graphs and patterns to pick the correct answers from the multiple-choice options—not even math whizzes come out of the exam feeling good about their responses, and no one understands the relevance of these "games" to the skills taught in law school. Maybe they're supposed to weed out the students who would otherwise ask questions such as, "Is there going to be a lot of math involved."

So, no, there was not going to be a lot of math involved, and I'd be interested to learn where that fellow female classmate of mine is today because there can be *a lot* of math involved when you are a lawyer. But, like everything else you do when you are first practicing, or even after years in the practice, you "fake it 'til you make it."

You pull out a calculator and work it out.

Your client wants to know how much he's getting in that accident settlement? Well, the attorney's fee is 1/3 the total settlement, so you need to know how to multiply numbers by .33.

Expenses are paid out of the total settlement so you need to know how to multiply the total settlement by .33 and then subtract the expenses out of what is left—and what remains is what the client gets.

A client wants to know whether he will qualify for a mortgage modification. You must determine what his gross monthly household income is, and then multiply that by a percentage as well.

Your client gets a letter from a debt collector adding on a $50 collection fee. You must be able to determine what percentage of the total debt the $50 fee is because in some states, that fee might be excessive and unlawful.

Even non-lawyers do a lot of math on a day-to-day basis. Making sure your paycheck is calculated correctly. Balancing a checking account. Determining whether the 8-ounce size is a better deal than the 12-ounce size. Math is everywhere in the real world.

Therefore, my advice to the young women in the audience was "Do the math. Don't be afraid of the math. Don't let the fact that you may not have been good at math in the 8th grade make you think you can't do math now. Realize that others out there will take advantage of people who seem to not know how to do the math. Buying a car, for example, is fraught with risk if you don't do the math on your own. The salesperson sure will do the math for you, and usually not to your advantage, if you don't know how to do the calculations on your own. If you avoid getting ripped off at the car dealer because you have crunched some numbers beforehand, you have less of a chance of needing someone like me to represent or advise you later."

The more hard-working people in financial distress I work with, the more I realize how important it is for the average person to tackle the math.

Do the math so that your money doesn't run out at end of the month.

Do the math so that you know whether you are getting the best deal.

Do the math so that you have money left over to invest for your future.

Do the math because there are no credit products out there designed to help you.

Do the math to show your 13-year-old self that you can do math and to show your kids that they can.

Get excited about doing the math. Look for chances to crunch numbers. Practice. Observe who else is good at math and who shies away from calculations. Then observe how much money the people who aren't afraid of the math have compared to those who are. Put yourself in situations where there is a lot of math involved. Life is only as complicated as the math, and so if you can do the math you're way ahead of the game.

8. Psychology

The more I work with people with debt, the more patterns I see. This has been an interesting way to observe that the psychology of having debt that can't be repaid is almost universal no matter what the demographic.

The biggest part of having too much debt that plagues the average American, especially when someone gets to the point where they can't repay it, is what I'll call the "boogeyman in the closet" phenomenon.

This is the fear that something terrible will occur *THE MINUTE* someone can't make a payment on their bills. The belief that missing a payment due date on a credit card is going to cause the sky to fall, it's going to cause instant public shame, *AND* on top of that, the boogeyman is going to come out of the closet or out from under the bed and *GET YOU*.

I know that this boogeyman is real because of the questions I get and the things people tell me based on their assumptions (or on the gobbledygook they read on the internet or that they get from their brother-in-law).

The boogeyman comes in the form of:

108

"If I miss my credit card payment, can they take my car?"

"If I'm overdue on my credit cards will they put a lien on my house?"

"Will my boss know?"

"Will they garnish my wages?"

"Will they take all my retirement?"

And, the big one,

"Can I be arrested?"

I'm heartbroken when I hear the fear that plagues people who can no longer make credit card payments, but am hopeful and encouraged, in a weird way, by their fear response. These questions signal to me genuine concerns about personal financial stability, reputation and a moral sense of right and wrong.

It shows that the average person, the majority of people, want to pay their bills, and want to pay them on time. I find that reassuring on many levels.

The answer to all the above questions is *No*. Some of those things can happen after several steps occur and usually only if someone ignores those steps or does not take advantage of their right to participate in those steps.

The state of mind that comes from the fear of not being able to pay bills is like that of a child hiding under the blankets in the dark while trying to fall asleep. The hard part is getting people to understand that they have control and that the boogeyman does not exist.

One of the first steps when counseling someone about their debt is to ascertain the level to which this fear is clouding their judgment and preventing them from being able to have a conversation about the real facts about their debt.

Their fears cause them to make less educated and less desirable decisions when it comes to dealing with their debt. They usually default to doing what they think they should do to not hurt their credit score. This includes doing what they think they should do to pay everyone at least something each month. When payment becomes difficult, they start having conversations with their creditors and think that what the creditors tell them (i.e., skip a month, or just pay $10 or $20 instead of the actual minimum payment) is official and overrides the requirement under the credit card agreement to make their actual payment. They are very vulnerable in this phase and even more so if they do skip payments and an account goes to collection.

By the time an account goes unpaid for about three months, a creditor will usually assign it to another company for collection. The exception is for car payments- not paying for more than a month or two puts you at serious risk of repossession of the vehicle, even if the creditor gives you verbal permission to make a late payment or a partial payment.

The good part about when a credit card account goes to collection is that by then the average person realizes there's no boogeyman. Their car is still in their driveway, there's no foreclosure sign in front of their house, their name isn't posted in front of town hall, and no one has shown up to put them in a stockade on their front

110

lawn. But a new phase has begun.

The typical debt collector in the U.S. may not actually even be in the U.S. The collection industry has consolidated considerably in the last decade (especially since the financial crisis of 2008-09) to where large percentages of unpaid accounts are sent to just a few collection companies. These are third party companies that are assigned portfolios of accounts, and the most common tactic for attempting to squeeze a payment or two out of the consumer is with phone calls.

Although the "fear of the boogeyman" phase is typically over by this point, the vulnerability and susceptibility remains. They're out of the woods, so to speak, but a sense of "I'm a bad person" takes over which makes them susceptible to abuse and harassment from debt collectors.

§

I talk about debt all the time. All. The. Time. That's what you do when you work with people who all have overdue credit cards or who are in foreclosure. They all have debt. Debt that has come tumbling down around them.

I talk about debt so much that I decided to talk about something different in a financial workshop I ran recently. Wealth. A novel subject. I have been holding monthly financial workshops for clients and anyone else who is interested. The week of this workshop I had a bad head cold, and it was hard to talk without descending into a coughing fit.

The usual agenda for my workshops is for the attendees to write out a few questions they have about various topics like dealing with debt collectors, credit scores and how to read a credit report, and whether they need to file for bankruptcy. But I wanted to talk about something else. Something that wasn't about me being in the role of teacher and the attendees as students. Something that didn't focus on the negative.

It went well. We tried to define wealth. Not easy, it turns out. We talked about what influences what we think of when we think about wealth. We talked about where we each feel we fall on a scale of 1 to 10, 1 being broke and 10 being wealthy.

The answers were touching- many people in the room said they felt close to a 1 in money but closer to a 10 in things like family life.

Then we talked about how to move from debt to wealth. And whether there really is a difference between the two (many people have wealth but don't have time to enjoy it, for example).

We came to no conclusions except that I think I helped diffuse the stress around the concept of debt. Talking about debt all the time, that has been my go-to stance—to demystify and weaken the power it has over the American psyche.

That's why I adopted *Got Debt?* from the milk industry's Got Milk? marketing campaign and used it on my business cards for many years. People would ask for my card, whether a potential client or just another business person wanting my contact info, and I'd say, "Sure!" and hand it to them with the black and white *Got Debt?* side up. I'd receive a laugh every time. It surprises people to see something negative like Debt substituted for the positive Milk. I even made up t-shirts one year with *Got Debt?* on the front. I gave them away to business contacts. One lawyer friend said when he'd go out for a run in the shirt people would pass him and say, "Yes, yes I do!"

There's no more reason to fear or be ashamed of debt any more than we fear or are ashamed of wealth. Like wealth, debt is fluid, it's a state of being but is not permanent. How we manage it is a decision we make. It doesn't determine what kind of person you are. I love the quote, "Being rich doesn't change who you are, it just emphasizes who you are. If you were nice when you were poor, you will be nice when you're rich"- and the corollary, that if you were an ass when you were poor you'll be even more of one when you have money.

People spend so much time beating themselves up about having debt, waste so many years and opportunities buried in shame over debt. Debt can be temporary but the state of mind that causes it, or prevents people from managing it or finding solutions to it is longer term and far more harmful to the average human.

I got a call from a debt collector one time. I allow clients to tell collectors to call me so they don't have to deal with the calls. Collectors rarely end up calling me so it's no big deal. The ones that do are interesting. It's always a different conversation, and fielding calls from these professional debt collectors makes me feel like the gladiator standing in the ring who has to knock down opponents one by one.

One collector was trying to convince me that my client had to pay, or else. I said, "He does?" and the collector responded, "Yes because debt never really goes away." I paused and considered that. I responded, "You mean spiritually? Because debt really can go away." That pretty much ended the call.

My point was that I acknowledged that you can carry debt with you as a psychological burden for as long as you want, but you don't have to.

It really can, and does, go away.

§

The first, and my favorite, kind of case I worked on as a consumer advocate was representing consumers harassed by debt collectors. There's a great little law called the Fair Debt Collection Practices Act, and like its name implies, it regulates the activities of third party debt collectors collecting personal, family or household debt. It's a federal law that tells debt collectors what they can and cannot do while collecting debts for others. Like all well-crafted laws, it is vague enough to have withstood the 40 years of changes in technology since its enactment. It uses phrases such as "including but not limited to" when defining types of harassment and abuse, so that if a collector does something similar to an activity described in the law, it can still be covered, and therefore prohibited, by the law. I get a kick out of a lot of aspects of working with the law, including the lingo used by collectors to refer to the law. One of the requirements when collecting consumer debt is the collector must indicate when it communicates with a consumer that "This is a communication from a debt collector. Any information obtained will be used for that purpose." Those in the industry call this the "Mini-Miranda", referring to the *Miranda* warnings required to be recited to someone being arrested for a crime.

One of the first cases under this law that came across my desk when I opened my own law office was from a woman who called and started the conversation with, "I'm calling because I just need to know if I'm going to jail." Well, that is an interesting way to start a conversation, and since I know that you can't be arrested for owing a debt, I asked her to explain to me why she was asking.

She said she had been having issues with her voicemail, and wasn't able to retrieve messages for several days or didn't realize she had any messages. When she finally listened to her messages, one was apparently from a debt collector that stated that a "Sheriff" was going to come to her job and "serve a warrant" because she had bounced a check and hadn't responded to the collector's phone calls. She returned the message and was informed the Sheriff was going to serve her the next day unless she could pay something like $785. I don't remember if she even knew what check this was or whether she even agreed that she owed anything; but the threat sounded to her like she was going to be arrested and so she asked me, "Should I tell my boss? I just want to let him know if I'm going to not be there because I'm going to be in jail." I think this was on a Monday or a Tuesday; she genuinely believed that by Thursday she would be behind bars.

I mention this story as an example of the susceptibility of consumers when they know they are late or behind on payments on their accounts. To her it made perfect sense that she "deserved" to be arrested and carted off to prison. I mention above that I am encouraged when someone feels an obligation to pay their bills; but this sense of obligation- that overshadows the average persons' belief that they have rights or that they can even question such a preposterous result- is fascinating. I am horrified by it and feel compelled to set people straight whenever I hear that they believe they should suffer like this over an unpaid bill. It's so interesting that they see their perceived wrongs as criminal when corporate debt and default on that debt is so rampant and no one is held liable, certainly not criminally.

Another interesting aspect of this shame or sense that they've done something morally wrong, if not committed a criminal act, is it's hard to get them to tell me about ALL the harassment they have experienced. It's very common for them to answer my questions, and even give me more detail when I end with "What else, did they say or do anything else?" After I have obtained what I think are all the facts, I research the location and reputation of the debt collector who engaged in the harassment, and then I draft up a lawsuit.

I usually test the waters by sending the lawsuit along with a cover letter informing the collector what they had done wrong and asking for a phone call to discuss my client's potential claim against the company. In many cases, the collector or a lawyer for the collector will contact me to discuss the facts of the case. Sometimes the collector doesn't really care to discuss the details and we settle quickly. Sometimes the collector or lawyer wants to go through all the claims and give me reasons why those actions do not violate the Act, justify why they occurred, or deny they occurred at all. I welcome these conversations.

I eventually saw a fascinating pattern emerge the more cases I handled where the collector wanted to hash out the details. In many instances, the collector would read from the call notes and tell me something I did not know happened. More often than not, it was something like this: "Did you know your client called my representative an asshole?" The first few times this happened, I was horrified. I feared this would hurt the case. After all, my client was supposed to be the victim. I would put the conversation with the collector on hold and contact my client.

I thought those conversations would end with me having to tell my client that our case was weakened by their behavior and that I was not likely to be able to settle, and that it wouldn't be worth pursuing the claim.

But what my clients almost always revealed really surprised me.

117

I would tell my client that I'd heard back from the collector and that they had informed me that they had it in their collection notes that the client had called the representative an asshole. The client's response? "Well, only after he called me a bitch!" Or some other equivalent expletive.

Why hadn't the clients told me about these exchanges? Over time I started chalking it up to the shame of having debt overshadowing the client's sense that they didn't have to be called names and transforming them into people who felt they deserved this treatment. Therefore, it wasn't worth discussing- it wasn't even abuse. To put it another way, to be called names, insulted, threatened, shamed and abused was considered a normal – and for some reason acceptable- consequence of having unpaid debt.

It became a pattern, and a pleasure, to call back the debt collectors and explain why my client had called the collector a bad name. And the cases would inevitably settle with little more discussion. Although I didn't like hearing that my client hadn't been 100% nice and polite when dealing with the collectors, I loved being able to remind the collectors that THEY were the ones regulated by Federal law, not my clients.

The client who was concerned about having to go to jail obviously did not go to jail. In the category of information clients almost don't tell me, at the very end of our initial call she said, "Oh, and I'm pregnant." If my lawyer brain hadn't already started calculating the settlement value of the threat of arrest and imprisonment, it was working overtime after that revelation. We settled for a healthy sum. But it wouldn't be the last time a debt collector made those kinds of false threats, and it wouldn't be the last time a client left out these important details.

§

Credit scores, despite everything, do serve an important purpose. Our economy has evolved to depend on quick, efficient access to credit and reliance on credit scores as an indicator of creditworthiness in-the-moment is vital to that purpose. However, when you start to depend on your score for your sense of well-being, it's time to look at credit scores a little more critically.

What are credit scores? They are a measure of your creditworthiness based on your historical use of credit. That is, if you have used credit "wisely" and have paid your creditors on time and stayed within credit limits, you are rewarded with a high credit score.

If you have fallen on hard times and have made late payments, skipped payments or have used up or "maxed out" all your available credit, you are punished with a low credit score.

A high credit score affords you the benefit of access to more credit and at lower rates of interest (so credit costs you less). The cost and availability of other products such as car insurance may also be influenced by credit score. Those with low scores are often seen as credit risks – if a low score is the result of having made late payments or having skipped payments, or of someone who is maxed out on other credit lines, then a new creditor is less likely to want to extend additional credit to that person.

Credit that is extended to those with low credit scores often comes with the high price of high interest rates and less available to borrow. Your score could be the difference between getting a $40,000 car loan at 4% and only qualifying for a $15,000 loan at 17%. If you need a large vehicle to accommodate your family size, this could be a problem. I also feel this is an example of how "it's expensive to be poor," a theme which I return to often when counseling clients.

The average American puts *a lot* of stock in their credit score. I can see why—nowadays, quick efficient access to credit is almost a requirement to go about your day. Inability to purchase a new vehicle when your car breaks down can prevent you from being able to get to work, and if you can't get to work you can't pay your bills… etc. etc.

Many people make financial decisions based on how their decisions will affect their credit. The most common example I see is the person whose credit cards are maxed out and who is paying hundreds and sometimes thousands of dollars in minimum payments each month. They do that so that no card is considered late and so they don't go over their credit limit. I recently met with a woman who has about $40,000 in outstanding credit card balances and pays about $1,400 per month in minimums (or an amount slightly above the minimum in an attempt to pay down the balance or to be able to keep using the card).

She came to me because she was suffering; paying her cards was causing extreme financial hardship. I asked her if she still used her cards; she said, yes, for basics like gas and groceries. In her case, I pointed out that making $1400 in minimum payments each month was taking cash she could be using to buy gas and groceries. My advice was for her to consider stopping paying her cards altogether.

The resistance to this advice was (and is) almost violent— "But that will kill my credit score! Then I won't be able to borrow any more money!" She was distraught—she loved the idea of having $1400 back in her pocket each month, but could not fathom a world in which SHE had a low credit score.

I understand. It's important to have a decent score at certain times of your life, like from age 18 to 88. That's a long time to need to worry about your credit score. But there are other times in life when your score really doesn't matter. There may be times in your life when you just can't afford to have a good credit score.

Let me explain what I mean. I usually call this theme "Credit Scores and Dandruff Shampoo." The premise is that credit scores are just a product developed and sold to the public. So were underarm deodorant, teeth whitening strips and dandruff shampoo.

My theory is that the market had room for these products, the need was there, and there were consumers just waiting for the products. Imagine a world in which *NO ONE* wears underarm deodorant. I can't, because I have always lived in a time and in places where attention to personal hygiene, specifically body odor, was a priority for most people.

But how did this come to be? Basic marketing campaigns. Someone at some point came up with a campaign that made those who had body odor feel ashamed for having body odor. But they didn't have to keep living that way! They could just buy this product— underarm deodorant!

Same with dandruff shampoo—the ad campaigns in the '70s and '80s that shamed people who had dandruff flakes scattered across their shoulders was a message I got loud and clear. And voila! Dandruff shampoo is very popular and you don't see nearly as many white flakes on clothing as in the past.

The newest obsession with personal hygiene is the idea that you must have white teeth. Hence the popularity of teeth whitening strips. They're everywhere, shaming those with less-than-snowy whites. I wonder what will be next.

Credit scores are very similar to these hygiene products: the market clearly had room for credit scores to be developed, there was a need, and there was a market. The similarity between hygiene products and credit scores is they both prey on your insecurities. Initially when scores were first developed, I doubt the public was even aware that scores existed and how they were being used. The Fair Credit Reporting Act wasn't enacted until 1970 and even that law doesn't exactly regulate credit scores—just the use of credit information by potential creditors, employers and others with a legitimate purpose for use of the information.

Once the public started to learn of the connection between their scores and their access to and cost of credit, the dam broke. Those with low scores were shamed, and those with high scores were finally receiving the "A grades" they worked for but never earned in school. The motivation to have a high credit score (whether to avoid the shame or to have access to the benefits) became as strong as that to avoid being the smelly one in the room, or the one with yellow teeth.

I try to put credit scores into this context and perspective so that the average person who hits a financial bump in the road does not overreact to having a low credit score. I often meet with people who self-select out of applying for certain jobs or even don't apply for work at all because they fear and assume their credit score may hold them back. While in a difficult job market they may be right, the assumption that a credit score is the most important thing about a person is just wrong.

Most credit reports and scores are not as bad as people think – recall my discussion elsewhere in this book about how people are afraid to look at their reports, but when I finally do, it's never as bad as they think it's going to be. I explain to new clients my theory that credit scores are like teeth whitening strips to show how they are just another product we've been sold. This may not succeed in wiping clean the reliance on scores for self-esteem right away, but it allows me to continue with a counseling session about credit without the score issue getting in the way.

I didn't realize until after talking with lots and lots of people about credit reports that I don't care what a client's credit score is. I do, however, care about accuracy of information in a credit report. Mainly because that is the standard under the law—if information on a credit report is accurate, then there isn't much you can do about it. But, equally importantly, I don't care about scores because I don't want people obsessing over that number, as if they are not good people if they don't have a good score. Remember, a credit score is not an adult grade.

The information on a credit report should reflect your use of credit, and if you have been lucky enough to not hit any major financial hurdles your score will reflect that. If you have, it's usually because of an unanticipated negative life event such as a layoff, illness, death of a spouse, parent or child, or divorce.

When I review a credit report I can almost always see exactly when the event occurred. The report shows when accounts began to be paid late or when payments stopped, so it's usually clear that a hardship occurred.

We shouldn't be ashamed when that happens, but thanks to credit scores and teeth whitening strips, many people will look negatively at themselves when their scores and their teeth aren't perfect.

§

Nothing against trolls - the fairy tale, Tolkien-type trolls, that is.

Big, strong, intellectually challenged, easily influenced, bumbling brutes that you sort of feel sorry for.

Then, though, there are internet trolls. The people who hang out online just waiting to pounce and provide an opinion that you are tempted to respond to but know you shouldn't. Don't look for mine, the exchange is long gone. He commented on a picture I posted on social media of me testifying before the Connecticut Legislature about our court foreclosure mediation program.

He was not a follower of my blog or social media, he just came out of the ether – asked a question I've heard a thousand times in a hundred different forms: "Why don't your clients just pay their bills?"

I did a quick click over to the troll's profile and saw that he was a member of a quasi-official offshoot of the Republican party and an ardent follower of the guy who would make us all great again. He also listed his occupation as "on Social Security Disability."

Be that as it may, I started thinking about a response to this type of self-righteous remark. I'm certain pointing out that my clients would pay if they could because no one likes being sued or foreclosed on would fall on closed ears. I also suspect that my other blog posts about the reasons people miss payments, how everyday things like divorce, job loss, or illness effect the best intentioned of us, would be scoffed at even while I pointed out the inevitability of one of those things happening over the course of an average mortgage (remember, 30 years is a long time).

But this guy displays neither empathy nor a sense of history.

125

Maybe if I thought it would be at all worth the time, I'd tell him this — that we should all care about the existence of the court's mediation program for homeowners in foreclosure, and we should care about those homeowners too, because foreclosed homes are blights on neighborhoods and are anchors pulling down everyone's home values.

That's it. Simple. Unless you are the only person in the country who believes that banks do a sparkling job of managing the homes they foreclose on, you want the people who love their homes to stay there.

That's it. Foreclosures hurt the community in a host of ways. If you're into draconian actions to punish delinquent homeowners because of whatever your personal hobgoblins are, you would do well to remember that somewhere along the line, you're harmed by every foreclosure that hits your community. You can demonize and blame or employ some empathy and work on prevention for everyone's benefit.

§

A friend of mine came by my office early one morning around Christmas. He lives in what is considered a "well-to-do" suburb of Hartford. Sipping his cup of coffee he told me this: he took a slightly different route out of town that morning and drove down a popular back road he hadn't taken in several months.

He was shocked and he doesn't shock easily. Over a short stretch, maybe half a mile, probably less, he counted five houses either abandoned or in foreclosure. Smack in the middle of nice homes with big yards and lots of trees. The other houses were so well maintained, the lawns neat and raked, that the empty houses stood out. They were eyesores.

They detracted completely from the rest of the street. My friend said it must have been an unhappy coincidence that that many houses were in foreclosure in such close proximity. There wasn't a water problem, the road wasn't about to be widened, this isn't an area afflicted by crumbling foundations. We looked up the numbers and it turns out the per-capita foreclosure rate in that town was much higher than surrounding towns. Apparently, home values in that nice, quiet small town with a good school system soared before the recession and hadn't fully recovered, leaving borrowers under water in their mortgages.

It was just a weird coincidence that there were so many on one street. He said he's glad he's just renting and that if he owned a house anywhere in town, he'd wonder what was going on and would be very concerned for his own home value. Half a street of abandoned homes is hardly conducive to real estate values.

Nor is a fading red Colonial with broken shutters, a partially collapsed garage, and two years' worth of leaves in the gutters.

It has always been my position, my belief, that we do everything we can to save homes in foreclosure because it goes beyond that one home, that one neighborhood. Foreclosed homes that sit untended destroy home values in the entire area. Lower home values lead to lower tax bases, which lead to hits on schools, infrastructure .... you get the picture.

As if to drive this home to me that Friday morning, an hour or so later I caught a short piece on NPR's Morning Edition. It was about the burned-out town of Paradise, California, the town decimated by the 2018 wildfires.

Some houses did survive the fires. Apparently it's not very expensive to make a house almost fire proof - special roofing, eaves, keeping fire resistant trees like maples while getting rid of flammable ones, keeping dead leaves and pine needles well away from the house.

NPR talked to some of the homeowners whose houses survived the fires. Lone houses in a sea of ashes. The predicament of an older couple whose home is survived, untouched, sums it up:

Their plan had been to sell in a couple of years so they could retire elsewhere. But who is going to buy their house now, in what remains of a ghost town?

Then I made the connection to another, slower-moving crisis hitting home here in Connecticut and parts of neighboring Massachusetts: crumbling home foundations. That topic can fill its own book.

Wildfires and other catastrophes fit into the example of my worst-case neighborhood scenario caused by the high foreclosure rate. There are a lot of people who also have the long-term goal of selling their homes to move away for retirement - who may face a similar fate, albeit at a much slower rate so you don't see it coming until it's too late.

§

A couple of scattered news articles that flitted across my news feed recently plus a 12:30 am TV commercial illustrate a new trend we need to be mindful of following.

First, the commercial: two friends hanging out when one gets a text, *YOUR CREDIT SCORE HAS CHANGED!* "Whoa," the other friend exclaims, "Why'd you get that?"

"I get instant updates on all my credit reports," replies the other. "Don't you know credit scores can change anytime?"

No, the friend didn't know that, but he's filled in now, credit scores can change any time, who wouldn't want to be on top of it? It's implied, not very subtly, that it's the height of irresponsibility not to track one's credit score 24/7. Luckily, XYZ company is there for you and, get this, it's free to start!

Next, the news items were about China where they are expanding their efforts to bring their brand of capitalism to the world through a system of "social credit scores" for their citizens, a program that has just started but is slated for a nationwide roll-out in 2020.

"Social credit." Your place in society is determined by your average score, the higher the average the better the car you can lease, community you can live in, job you can apply for. I first became aware of the concept like a lot of people did, through the Netflix and BBC show, *Black Mirror*. The first episode of the third season, *Nose Dive*, was about a not so distant future where every one of our social interactions, from buying a coffee, to standing in line in an airport, to who you interact with in the office, are rated on a 1 to 5 scale. Another perspective on this concept is explored through an episode of *The Orville*, a sort of modern Star Trek by the creator of *Family Guy*.

I have already felt the sting of such a system myself when I learned that I only have a 4.75 rating (out of 5) on Uber, the ridesharing app, which means that some driver did not find that I was an ideal passenger. Humph.

It's scary in that "it can easily happen" sort of way that China seems ready to turn into reality. The whole, "Let's grade everyone on everything they do" motif feeds into a "Let me see what I'm rated today" that looks a lot like Americans' obsession with credit scores (and now, apparently, smaller things like their Uber ratings, apparently).

The reason this system can be widely adopted in a place like China is they don't have as much credit, if any, in their non-Capitalist economy as Americans do. We can be graded on our use of credit but they can't. The powers that be found something else to grade its citizens on.

That's not why I'm writing about this. What all this did was remind me, vividly, of a constant theme of this book: the effect shame and embarrassment have on the average American, and its power to control us.

We have long been conditioned to be mortified by a dropping credit rating, an unpaid bill, a certified letter or collection call, a law suit, a foreclosure, anything about money that negatively reflects on us.

I have to constantly explain this to clients-- what they are going through is happening to other people, lots of people, right now and all the time. That there's no reason to be embarrassed or shamed, just take care of the issue in the best possible way and moving on with life. No one who matters is judging you, credit scores can be repaired, the banks, lawyers, court clerks, judges, and collection companies are all on to the next case, there are no institutional memories.

They have a hard time accepting that. Take a step back and look at how effective our society is at keeping control based on financial situation and credit score.

Embarrassment and shame and the other dozen related emotions are unfortunately very effective in inhibiting people from seeking help at the time professional help is most needed. This goes for foreclosure defense as well as family law issues, dealing with the IRS and a host of other matters.

Good lawyers have seen everything in their area of practice, they deal with everything, they will not judge. Most of all, they won't give you a score or rate you on or off social media.

§

I started training for a half marathon not long before starting to put this book together. I went from not running much ever in my adult life into a full-out endurance training program, and going from couch to completing my first half marathon in 96 days.

Following a workout calendar was key. Training was going great. I ran a 15k (just over 9 miles) about two months after starting training. I was sore at the finish but continued toward my 13-mile goal. But when I set out to tackle my first-ever 12-mile training run, I found myself struggling by mile four. I have several friends who, at various times in their lives, have trained long and hard for serious athletic goals. I held out to mile five before calling one of those friends, a fellow attorney who had been a semi-pro athlete and was also a runner.

Think of the lifeline option in *Who Wants To Be A Millionaire*. He was my phone-a-friend. I tried his cell phone at 7 on that warm Sunday morning. He didn't answer. But he called me back about 20 minutes later. At this point I was at about mile 7, struggling and crying.

Two seconds into the call he simply said, "Oh, you've just hit the wall. It's normal."

The Wall. I didn't see it coming. I had talked to him about the ups and downs, the disappointments and epiphanies I'd had learning to run distance. But as for a Wall, I had no idea. I asked for an explanation, but he had none except, "Well, you know what it is now and you've hit it."

He was right. I had never felt anything like that, ever. It sure was something. It wasn't fear. It wasn't fatigue. It wasn't self-doubt. It was weird– anger, frustration and self-pity. Those were the bricks in my wall. A wise person once said, "Go out for a run, it will tell you who you are." She got that right.

It was also a simple decision point – quit or go on. Going forward would surely hurt, quitting would hurt in an entirely different way … and for a lot longer, of that I was sure.

I had been told – by the same friend who couldn't really describe the wall – that breaking through it feels great, eventually. He coached me through it, gave me license to walk for a bit, then said, "Just get home." It wasn't pretty, but I didn't cut that run short and I got home. I wasn't proud, but I didn't let the wall stop me. Knowing that felt great.

Hitting the wall was quite the experience and it occurs to me that homeowners go through this same process as they near foreclosure. They work, work, work, negotiate, deal with banks, keep things moving, then hit a wall. It could be when instead of helping, the bank files for foreclosure. It could be a number of other things.

A big part of my job is letting homeowners know that there is life beyond the wall, they just have to break through. When you hit the Wall it's not over. There's a second act and it can be rewarding . . . but you must keep going.

§

Speaking of running and training.

Sir Roger Bannister died in 2018 at age 88. He was the man who broke the four-minute mile in 1954. Accolades flowed from around the world, his familiar story told and retold: a sub four-minute mile was impossible; doctors and sports trainers believed breaking the four-minute barrier would kill the runner; Bannister, a great cross-country runner, refused to listen to any of it and simply ran his guts out one cool, overcast day and proved all of them wrong.

Good story, but not really true and, as these things usually go, not as good as the real story. One of the best articles I've read immediately after Bannister's death was by Malcolm Gladwell, *The Ordinary Greatness of Roger Bannister.*

Ordinary greatness. Interestingly, Roger Bannister was not an elite runner when he did the "impossible." He was a very good cross-country runner and a competitive miler - mostly because he was tall, lanky, and had a great stride.

He was running for a club but only sporadically because his real job was full-time medical student. He trained during his lunch hours. Once, after a particularly bad week of training he took off with a friend to hike in Scotland. Just to get away from school and running.

On the face of it, Rudy of *Rudy* fame showed more single-minded intensity over a longer period to make his 15 second appearance for Notre Dame than Bannister did in pursuit of sports immortality.

Or did he? Roger Bannister knew exactly what he was doing every step of the way to 3:59.4 for the simple reason he planned every step. Literally.

As a good, solid runner, Bannister knew what it took to run a four-minute mile. Any halfway decent runner, then and now, knows what it takes because every halfway decent runner can run a 4 minute pace for at least fifty yards.

A four-minute mile is 15 miles per hour. The mile is symmetric, four laps around the track. At a minute each, you have a four-minute mile. In between medical school classes, Bannister planned it all out. He studied the effects of 15 mph on the body and made adjustments to his diet, breathing, stride; he redesigned his shoes (at the time the spikes alone weighed more than track shoes today) and figured out a greasy formula that kept track cinders (all tracks were cinder tracks then) from sticking and clotting his spikes.

Then he plotted the race. It wasn't about running just under a minute, four times over, it was about not being exhausted at the end and being able to utilize his long stride and big kick to maximum advantage ... which meant figuring out the precise, optimum time to do so.

Go too early, run out of gas at the end; go too late, finish over four minutes with wasted gas still in the tank.

There was also the matter of the first laps and keeping, without going too far over or too far under, that one minute or so pace. It was 1954, times were kept by hand-held stopwatches, there were no scoreboards showing the time in illuminated digits. How, then, to insure he kept the pace he settled on in the first laps? He solved that problem by using "rabbits" - friends who would pace him before dropping off.

The rest, of course, is history. He executed his plan and replicated that success three months later in Vancouver against Australian John Landry. Bannister improved his time to 3:58.9; Landry, also broke the four-minute mark for the second time. Bannister then retired from running to devote all his time to becoming a neurologist.

By now you know where I'm going with this – it's all about planning. Especially when you have a legal issue. Though it may not seem it to someone facing a foreclosure, or in the middle of a contract dispute, or a contentious divorce, or ... well, you get the picture, take a moment to sit back, breathe, and plan with your lawyer. The big picture - 3:59.4 – and the little things – keeping your cleats from clogging.

That way, we can all achieve ordinary greatness. Your victory may not be newsworthy or record-breaking, but we may just save your house, and for you and your family, that's historic.

9. Collections and More

The Fair Debt Collection Practices Act was enacted to prevent the oppressive acts debt collectors (companies and their individual employees) from using unfair pressure tactics to induce people to make payments. There's a strong anti-competitive purpose to the Act too—that is, if only some collectors comply and use fair, lawful means, they may not collect as much as collectors who use harassing, abusive and oppressive means to collect. Most consumers I spoke with who have dealt with debt collectors tell me that you can catch more flies with honey and that they would have offered to pay had the collector been nicer. But overall, strongarm tactics seem to work often enough that some collectors make it their M.O.

Enter the voice message worth thousands.

Few clients who are abused by a debt collector for the first time call lawyers. Most who find their way to lawyers are not looking to file suit, they just know something happened that was "off" and are looking to have that sentiment validated. Maybe they want to see if they deserve, and can get, an apology. I am usually the one that tells them that there's a law, that the collector broke the law and that they may be able to recover some money for the harassment. Most of the people I speak to then tell me that they're not looking for money, they even say I can KEEP any money I get, they just want the abuse to stop. This is another common pattern that I see handling collection harassment cases, and one that proves that people who can't pay their bills aren't deadbeats and bad people. It really isn't about the money for the client; it just wasn't fair and they want the balance righted back to level if possible.

One day a new client called with a complaint about a collector. The events that lead up to the offense go something like this: Phone rings, client picks up and it's a collector looking for a payment. Client can't talk, her son was just dropped off by the babysitter and she forgot to tell her something so she ends the call and goes out the front door to talk to the babysitter. At that moment, the collector called back. Her 8-year-old son picked up the phone. The collector asks to speak to his mother and the son tells him she can't pick up the phone and ends the call. The collector calls back and by this time the mother is there, tells her son not to pick up, and the answering machine picks up. The collector leaves a message that included the following: "Mrs. ___, I know you're there. I know you're hiding behind your little child. People like you shouldn't even have children if you can't even pay your bills…"

The challenge in handling this case, in the early 2000s, was getting the message off the client's little answering machine tape and into a format I could share with the collector and its attorney. I think it involved her bringing in her answering machine, and me holding up a digital Dictaphone to the machine to record it. Then I had to figure out how to get the recording into a format I could attach to an email. By the time I had drafted the harassment suit and sent it out with a settlement demand, I had figured out the technology issues so I was ready. The collector's attorney asked me to prove that the collector said what we say he said, and I just had to attach the recording to an email. The suit settled quickly.

Oh, and by the way, this client was pregnant, too.

§

Collectors are persistent. Collectors take it personally when you don't answer your phone, when they can't reach you, when they think you're out there spending all your money - *THEIR* money—on frivolous things like food and medication instead of agreeing to send in a portion of your paycheck. Some collectors are just a guy in his basement with a list of names and account numbers he bought.

If they get a hit and someone agrees to make a payment, they usually make a profit, no matter how small the payment. So any time they can't reach someone, any time someone just doesn't pick up the phone because they know it's a collector and they know they don't have any money to pay, the collectors get resentful. Like in the other examples I discuss, they say some nasty things. However, the pattern with collectors is the more blatantly they violate the Act, the more likely they are to be one of the guys working out of his basement; so not a legitimate collector and not following the law. And not so likely to be on the map.

I met with a potential client who had a Hispanic last name. I'll call her Rosa Diaz. She too had a recording of a collector. She had been receiving calls for a few weeks and she came to my office with her daughter because she was distressed about the calls. She couldn't pay the account and wanted the calls to stop. She didn't know who the calls were from—she hadn't received a letter even though collectors are supposed to send out notices, so we didn't know who to send a letter to to demand that the calls stop which is your right under the Act. They brought in a recording of one of the messages. It went something like this: "Mrs. Diaz, or Mrs. Rodriguez, or Mrs. Ortiz, or whatever your name is, pick up the phone. We need to speak to you about an important matter…"

The Fair Debt Collection Practices Act outlines what collectors are not supposed to do while collecting debts. Those prohibitions include using any harassing, oppressive or abusive means to collect a debt. I thought the rattling off a list of common Hispanic last names and saying "Or whatever your name is" was a strong violation of the act - after all, it sounded offensive to me and the client was offended.

I have been invited several times to the local law school to speak to the consumer law class about the Act. I prepare a list of things collectors have done and said to my clients over the years and I use it to help the students identify violations and discuss how and why these things violate the Act. I added the Mrs. Diaz example to the list and got a very interesting response. About half the students didn't think it was a violation. We referred back to various sections of the Act that prohibit the use of language the purpose of which is to harass a consumer, we analyzed the sections that regulate misrepresentations and other deceptive statements, but some of the class just didn't see how this message violated the law. I thought it was one of the more obvious violations on the my list of examples. I am still surprised at the response I received from that class and continue to be impreesed with the complexity of this little law.

So, what happened? Did it settle or did a judge determine that it was harassment? As is common with this type of blatantly rude, if not violative, collection activity, we could not identify the collector and so we could not bring the case. Mrs. Diaz was left with a bad taste in her mouth and so was I. But the Act doesn't prohibit that.

§

In my opinion the Mrs. Diaz example, at the very least, could have fallen under the "least sophisticated consumer" standard used to break the tie in borderline harassment cases. This is a judge-made standard developed in response to debt collectors attempting to use the "the consumer should have known better" excuse to get out of liability for their bad acts. Under the least sophisticated consumer standard, even a lawyer who sues debt collectors, but who finds herself the subject of abusive debt collection activity, can have a claim against a collector. That is, even though there is something about you that should make you "sophisticated," such as having a 4-year degree, a law degree or even lots of experience with debt collection, if the activity would have offended or would have been considered abusive by the LEAST sophisticated consumer then the activity can be considered a violation.

How does this help? It makes it so that the measure is not how much a particular individual consumer is affected, but if any consumer would be affected by abuse. In an arena where the playing field is not level—because the boogeyman has softened consumers' resolve, because they already feel like they deserve to be harassed merely because they are late on their bills (I venture to say it's a response that we adopt in exchange for paying bills—that is, if paying bills insulates us from abuse, not paying bills opens the floodgates of abuse), a collector cannot pick and choose when the same comment or action is abusive. If the standard therefore is that if the comment or action could possibly offend anyone, then the collectors need to be sure that they don't say anything out of line. Obviously, this doesn't prevent them from crossing the line, or coming close to the line to test the waters. The Mrs. Diaz example I think falls squarely in the arena of harassment especially because she herself was offended and felt that the collector only left that message to induce her to respond with the aim of collecting something from her.

The standard also allows for the various ways we perceive things based on where we are in life. If you're in the "fear of the boogeyman" phase of dealing with your inability to pay your bills, then you may be more apt to interpret a collector's statements as abuse. There has to be a logical connection between the abuse and how it could fit into the prohibitions in the Act; not just any fragile consumer can create abuse where it really does not exist. The "eggshell plaintiff" standard is one we're taught in law school—if you are in a minor fender-bender and the other guy already has a weakness and you make it worse, you are liable for all his harm, not just the minimum that would have logically flowed from a similar fender-bender. There is a time and place for "eggshell" qualities to come into play—such as a consumer who has been abused who is also pregnant and is told she shouldn't even have children. The least sophisticated consumer standard is an attempt to codify a point beyond which a debt collector may not go. It's hard to predict when something will cross the line, and collectors are good at trying to move the line.

§

I recently met with a woman who told me she hasn't been sleeping.

She's been having nightmares where people from her mortgage company come to her house and move her stuff out. She calls out

"Stop!" but either no sound comes out, or they can't hear her, or they ignore her.

I'm going to go out on a limb and guess that she had these dreams because representatives from her mortgage lender were calling about her missing payments.

That's understandable, they're just trying to get paid. It's their job to collect payments. If it stopped at, *"When can we expect your payment?"* it would be acceptable.

But they don't. They try to induce any kind of payment they can get out of her by advising that if they start to foreclose she'll have to move out of her house in 30 to 60 days. That's basically it: "Okay, don't pay, we will file for forelcosure, you're out of the house before the new season of *Chicago Med* starts."

There's pretty much zero truth behind that threat as it applies to foreclosures in my state. Since most every homeowner behind on their mortgage is stressed out, the bank's threat/misrepresentation is very powerful. Nightmare-inducing, in fact.

There may well come a time in any unresolved foreclosure when the homeowner is 30-60 days from having to vacate the property. That time is nowhere near being two months behind on payments.

One of the most satisfying parts about my job is counseling homeowners on just how long a foreclosure can take. I get to tell them about due process and how long they still have to live in their homes. It's always months and months longer than they think.

§

A friend of mine received a phone call on his cell phone from an unidentified Rhode Island number. He went to college in Providence, has friends there, so he answered.

This is what he got – "Hi, Mr. Loman, this is an attempt to collect a debt, anything you say can and will be used against you... Can you confirm the last four digits of your social security number?"

"No."

"Is it 5555?"

"Perhaps."

"Okay, well, I have an account here from Verizon, you owe twelve hundred dollars."

"I've never had a Verizon account."

"Well, sure, but it could also be from -"

"Could be?"

"From any one of the following companies now part of Verizon ...". The guy then read off a very long list of companies, a list that pretty much summed up the telephone industry of the 21st Century.

"No," my friend answered.

"No? Whattaya mean, no?"

"I don't owe anything to anyone on that list."

"Says here you do."

"Then it's wrong."

"Look, Biff, I have it right here and -"

My friend has a law degree and a long history of dealing with total BS, so it finally hit him to ask, "Wait a second, what's the date on this supposed debt?"

The guy on the phone fumbled around, Biff could hear papers being shuffled, murmurs of other voices from the boiler room, then, "Yeah, got it here, 2003."

"You're calling me about a twelve-year-old debt?"

"Well, no, see, we just received it -"

"Yeah, well, how awful for you, have a nice day, don't ever call again."

Done. Or almost, because then Biff Loman did a reverse number lookup on the "collection agency" that had never identified itself. The number was associated with a manufacturing firm in Pawtucket – where Biff worked and lived in the summers in college – that went out of business in the '90s (Biff said it was hardly in great shape when he was there in the '80s). This is known as "spoofing" and it's hardly a sign you're dealing with any kind of stand up, legitimate company.

There's little doubt this was a company that buys up old debt for pennies (if that) on the dollar and then tries to collect on it. They are hardly known for the gentility of their subsequent collection activities.

My friend had, in fact, just dodged a deep, black hole of hurt. As pointed out by Jake Halprin in *Paper Boys: Inside the Dark, Labyrinthine, and Extremely Lucrative World of Consumer Debt Collection*, an amazing, jaw-dropping *New York Times* article – old debt is resold over and over again and is a spectacularly profitable industry. The problem is, Halprin explains:

> A gamut of players — including debt buyers, collectors, brokers, street hustlers and criminals — all work together, and against one another, to recoup every penny on every dollar. In this often-lawless marketplace, large portfolios of debt — usually in the form of spreadsheets holding debtors' names, contact information and balances — are bought, sold and sometimes simply stolen.

If you are coerced into paying anything toward one of these so-called debts, you only accomplish one thing – the collector makes about 1000% profit and your payment or any settlement agreement you enter into might never be reported to anyone and the account may be sold again … and again.

These guys collect hundreds of millions of dollars in what is essentially a completely unregulated, underground industry that profits by manipulating our fears.

§

I spend a lot of time explaining to people that it's not personal. The fact that they owe an overdue balance on a credit card or their mortgage is not perceived as a personal offense by the creditor. It isn't. Maybe a creditor has its collection department contact you, and maybe the representative in that call center makes you feel like it's personal, but that call center rep must make at least 100 calls per shift and the calls are all the same. It's just a job for that person. Your file is assigned to them by their computer, even your phone number is dialed by the computer, and they really don't care about the reasons you are unable to pay. They are similar reasons as the other 99 people they have called or will call in any given day.

Consumers I work with, however, seem to want it to be personal. Remember Mrs. Goldman who with her husband had over $95,000 in credit card debt? She thought it was personal. I understand that-- they have stopped paying certain bills and can't believe that no one cares! This flies in the face of everything they have been raised to believe. If you don't do your homework, you're bad. If you show up late to work, you're bad. If you don't work hard, you're bad. If you don't pay your bills, you're bad. So how is it not personal when you don't pay your bills?

First, there are SO MANY people who can't pay their bills that no one individual call center representative could possibly muster the energy to take all his or her targets' inability to pay personally. That would just require time and energy that the average human does not possess. The call center rep may be trained to use certain phrases to make you feel bad about your inability to pay, but they don't actually *CARE*. They have the same conversation 100 times per day; after half a day, you wouldn't care either. In fact, the rep probably does sympathize with all the people he calls each day, but just can't say so.

More likely than not, he is just numb to all the sad stories of hardship. He may be behind on his own bills too.

Some people think they are targeted or singled out. They feel like no one is helping them save their house or lower their monthly payments so the bank MUST be out to get them. I even have people tell me how they suspect the bank wants *THEIR* house, because it's such a nice house in such a nice neighborhood, and therefore the bank is refusing to help them keep their house.

These are average people with very average houses, for the most part, so it must be the stress of possible foreclosure that brings out a response that ranges from paranoid to narcissistic. Please understand, the people calling don't want your house. They are not out to get you. That's not even a decision they can make or recommend.

It's their computers that do that – they calculate when you're behind by X amount, and so your file is put into a system that moves forward unless you can stop it by catching up on your payments. That's it. There is no individual at a mortgage company or credit card company making decisions about any individual borrower or customer.

Except, perhaps, the smaller local lender. This is the lender with billboards up on country roads inviting residents of the community to buy their first home or to refinance away from that big national lender. This is the lender that uses local sports heroes or other small-town celebs to promote their products. This is also the lender who may partner with a state or federal programs to help working class homebuyers.

You'd think that this lender would be kinder and gentler on borrowers when those borrowers eventually fall behind - after all, this bank paints itself as a community builder, one that seeks out the distressed borrower to apply for a home mortgage to begin with. When I say that lenders don't take things personally when it comes to customers who fall behind-- I was *NOT* referring to these local lenders. They *DO* take it personally. I have no idea why.

It doesn't make sense because these small local lenders know they are helping many financially fragile first-time home buyers. These are borrowers who typically earn less than the average homeowner and who need down payment assistance programs. They typically do not have a college education or a secure career path. There's so much love at the beginning of this relationship, there's a lot of patting each other on the back going on at the small bank who gets the single mother who earns an hourly wage into a home.

They gladly take her payment each month, that is, until she needs a break and asks to pay late. Or has to skip one month because she missed a week of work while home with a sick child. Or because she got hurt at her waitressing job and her disability benefits won't come through for 90 days…

Then the small bank gets indignant. "How can she ask for such a thing? Didn't she learn anything when we helped her get this mortgage—didn't she learn that those payments need to be paid on time each month?" (Pay your mortgage on time or you're bad.)

You insult them with your request for help. You offend them when you ask that your bank treat you like a human with human problems. You confuse them with your proposed payment plan to pay half the payment this month, and make up the unpaid half over the next three months…

They are bankers, they told you you could afford the mortgage so you can pay it. So, NO. How dare you ask for a break. You insult them, and they take that very personally.

There is at least one small local lender in my area that fits this exact profile. Their marketing campaign speaks of how great they are for putting you into your first home. They use at least one local hero athlete in their ads. They extoll the virtues of their partnership with the state to help with down payments to maximize homeownership among people who never thought they could qualify. They are based in a small, working-class city and its target demographic is the lower-income worker who is susceptible to financial hardship.

When I get a call from someone looking for help because they're in foreclosure and I hear this lender's name, I groan. I know what this is going to be like. It's going to be like dealing with a fifth-grade girl whose best friend started flirting with her boyfriend.

Seriously. You'd think my clients had personally insulted the president of the bank on national television; it's as if my client had stolen the president's wallet or killed his cat. The shock and dismay that one of their financially fragile borrowers dared to fall behind on their mortgage is bizarre. As if they couldn't see it coming lending to people who could never have afforded a mortgage without this lender's programs. The contrast between the love at the beginning and the hate when their customers need help just makes no sense to me.

The fights they decide to fight make no sense either. I recently represented a family who was *this close* to being kicked out of their home after foreclosure. The family had come to me after title had already passed back to the small local lender described above. The family and I worked out a plan where I would ask the court for more time before the family had to move out, and in the interim they would file for bankruptcy protection.

That all worked but the family still hadn't been able to save up enough money to rent an apartment by the time the bankruptcy was over and their protection ended. The bank filed another request to eject the family from the home, and the forced move-out was scheduled for 7am the Tuesday after a national holiday, one of the ones that falls on a Monday. Hearings are only one day per week (Mondays, unless Monday is a holiday and then Tuesdays).

The week before (she had very little notice), the wife came to my office and we discussed her options. She just needed another month to save up a security deposit and move her family to the apartment she had lined up. I said I might be able to get her that much more time if the lender's lawyer would agree. I gave him a call and he asked if she had a signed lease. I had to tell him no, because she didn't have the deposit and first month's rent saved up yet. I asked him if I filed a motion to stay the ejectment would he agree to postpone the ejectment to have it argued in court at the Tuesday hearing (as there was no court on Monday). He said no. I asked if he would agree to move the ejectment just to Wednesday, so that my motion for stay could be heard in court on Tuesday, and he said no, you'll have to somehow get it in front of a judge before the 7am Tuesday ejectment.

All I was asking for was to get the family three more weeks to comfortably move into an apartment. Or one more day to have a fair hearing in open court with a judge. The small local lender's lawyer's failure to agree to any of that meant the family had to start moving their own things right away or the state marshal in charge of the ejectment was going to arrive at dawn on Tuesday morning with a moving truck and crew to force the family out and put their belongings into storage, whether they had somewhere to go or not.

By not agreeing to delay the ejectment <u>one day</u>, the lawyer for this little local lender forced me to request that a judge review my motion in chambers with no argument because the court was closed that Monday and doesn't schedule hearings last minute on Thursdays or Fridays. The lawyer did not give any good reason to object to a one-day delay-- it just felt like he was taking it personally that this family wanted even a minute more in the house.

In the end, the family did their best to move out over the holiday weekend. The wife ended up in the hospital with heart palpitations due to the stress and was still in the hospital the morning of the ejectment.

That Tuesday morning, I was in court on other matters. The lawyer for the lender was there also! When he was done arguing his cases I got up and held the door for him as he wheeled his briefcase out of the courtroom. Inside I was thinking, "You creep! We <u>could</u> have had a hearing today because we are both here in court!"

Instead I smiled and simply said "Hi." His response: "We have nothing to talk about," and he walked away.

I suddenly had a flash back to my best friend in fifth grade telling me the same thing when I started flirting with her boyfriend.

§

I never know why attorneys choose the area of law they opt to practice in. I wonder, of course, why I chose one path, the path of always working on the side of the consumer, and why others chose the complete opposite path- where their work has at its core the goal of making consumers suffer.

I have met attorneys who make me think, *"If only this person were working FOR consumers instead of against them, we'd have a powerful advocate on our side."*

Mostly though I just take my opponents as they come. I assume they fell into the work they are doing the way I did: someone hired them out of law school and that was that. The career goals of those who went in the direction of collecting debts were obviously not in line with mine. A different moral compass had to guide them, no matter how high their student loans.

When people asked me what I wanted to do after graduation, I used to say, "I want to save the world." I looked for jobs that went along with that.

I can't envision the law student who would answer, "I want to be a debt collector someday."

I've written about my first job out of law school, but what I haven't really addressed is *the other side.*

While helping clients defend against collection lawsuits, I got to know all the debt collection law firms that brought all the suits.

This is about one in particular.

One of the firms I dealt with the most when I began representing middle-class consumers defend against credit card collection suits was a relatively small outfit down in New Haven.

The owner was an older man whose take-no-crap and believe-no-excuse attitude lent itself well to being a debt collector. Think someone out of a Dickens or Steinbeck novel.

The firm had just a few associates and paralegals but handled thousands of files at the small claims and superior court levels. The attorneys and support staff followed the owner's lead and all were particularly hard on consumers. They were unrelenting when it came to trying to work out settlements or giving extensions when my clients just wanted to buy time.

They would not do it.

Instead, they would place judgment liens on consumers' homes once they obtained judgments, which is permitted, and took the extra step of actually attempting to foreclose on those liens, forcing consumers to defend yet another lawsuit and to either refinance their house, if they could, or borrow from retirement funds to repay the relatively small judgments, or else risk losing their homes.

For some reason, one day I typed the firm's name into Google. I don't remember why or what I was looking for.

I went deep with the Google search. Somewhere on page 5 or 6 of the results I came across an article about the firm in the *Wall Street Journal* from 2002 detailing an investigation into the firm's practices.

Only at the time of the investigation, the firm wasn't collecting old, unpaid credit card debt. Its business was collecting medical debt owed to two local, prominent hospitals.

The scandal the article described was multi-layered: first, the hospitals had "free bed funds" available and were supposed to inform low-income patients they could apply for these funds to help pay for their medical costs. Although millions of dollars were available, only a fraction were ever applied for because the hospitals weren't actually informing its patients about the program. The hospitals instead allowed medical costs to accrue and go into collection.

The hospitals then referred the unpaid bills to the New Haven firm with the tough owner. The firm was apparently using the same heavy-handed collection tactics that I knew to be its trademark: strict demands for payment, followed by lawsuits and judgments, then liens on property and then foreclosure of those liens.

The *WSJ* article detailed cases where low-income patients who should have been offered assistance were billed, then sued for the balance and many eventually lost their homes to foreclosure when they could not pay the judgments. A sad, shameful outcome given the circumstances.

This firm that did all the debt collection was revealed to be the hospitals' highest paid vendor, above any doctor, surgeon or any other outside service provider. Wow.

The article was picked up by the local paper and caused public outrage and shaming of the hospitals, who were forced to change their practices. In the wake and as token proof of the change in their policies, the hospitals fired the firm.

The law clinic at the law school who discovered the travesty and who took on the defense of the low-income patients, pro bono, was lauded for its work and to this day can singlehandedly take credit for ceasing abusive collection practices by hospitals, forcing hospitals all across our state to publicize the availability of free bed funds as well as changing the law on interest rates that can be charged on hospital bills.

By time I had set up my shop, all this was old news.

What I realized, sitting there in my office, reading and re-reading the article, was the victims of the hospitals and its lawyers' collection tactics were low income and therefore qualified for the law clinic's pro bono services. They also qualified for the public's sympathy.

What happened to the law firm? It turns out that if you do work for a prominent client such as a community or university hospital that has (or is forced to develop) a corporate conscience, you have to align your morals with that institution. Once the hospitals started behaving, their collectors had to also. The firm I'm talking about had to be thrown out with the bathwater, and we'll never know if they were given the opportunity to align their practices with the hospitals' new ones. Other than losing this business, the firm wasn't punished or reprimanded.

No other hospitals hired them, of course. How did they survive? They just pivoted. They had the infrastructure in place to engage in collection activity, it would be a shame to let it go to waste. So they just found new clients: third-party debt buyers of unpaid credit card debt, with names like Unifund and Midland Funding, who were suing little old ladies and lots of others.

So what, why did I care? There's nothing illegal or improper about that.

So long as they were working for hospitals, however, there was some kind of regulation, modulation of their actions, at least once the public was made aware of what was going on.

That disappeared when it came to this firm engaging in the collection of old credit card debt.

Compare a low-income hospital patient who qualifies for financial assistance with the typical person who has unpaid credit card debt. The former is seen as a victim; the latter was wealthy enough, at least at some point, to qualify for a credit card.

On the surface, it can be concluded that people who need free-bed funds to pay medical bills are in the lower class, and those with credit card debt are middle- or upper middle-class.

Medical debt usually results from illness or other circumstances beyond a patient's control. Credit card debt is a symptom of spending beyond one's means.

I don't need to explain who is the more sympathetic of the two.

Look at it this way, which one would a judge feel more sympathy for? Which one qualifies for pro-bono legal help?

It hit me then - by pivoting from collecting medical debt to collecting credit card debt, this law firm essentially went underground. They went from doing work that was publicly scrutinized involving sympathetic victims to doing work that involved a demographic that doesn't qualify for legal aid and whom society sees as having brought their own problems on themselves.

Now the firm could engage in the same practices, including foreclosing on homes, and no one would bat an eyelash. And no one did. From a business perspective, it was brilliant. But if it was you who hit hard times and found yourself on the wrong side of a credit card collection suit, it could be game over.

This story isn't really about the law firm. It's about how we see each other, our neighbors and fellow community members, how we determine who merits our sympathy based on the type of debt they have.

The firm benefits from the public shaming we impose on our fellow citizens, the judgment we pass based on how we feel others should live their lives, what decisions they should have made. The firm benefits from the fact that the consumers they sue don't qualify for legal aid. No law school clinic is going to take up the cause of the unemployed software engineer whose credit card balances are overdue - the middle class, even when unemployed, don't typically qualify for pro bono help. Add the element that the guy also doesn't think he can afford an attorney, because there are few if any around who know how to offer him services at an affordable rate.

People in his situation don't get an ounce of sympathy from the rest of us. And so the firm can just keep on going. In recent years, since the economy crashed, this firm has backed off on foreclosing on the judgment liens, but they are still bringing thousands of cases to collect credit card balances.

We can't blame them. They're just doing a job, albeit in a way that makes people suffer, people who have nowhere to turn for legal help. The average middle-class American, though, believes that people should pay their bills, and so not even their neighbors, family or friends have sympathy for them. A sentiment from which the firm profits.

I want the firm to be ashamed of what it's doing. But first, shame on the rest of us.

§

I don't know about you, but sometimes my idea of fun is helping my clients to get judgment liens paid off. Don't judge- it's kind of a cool challenge and can be really satisfying. Taking care of liens has been a satisfying part of being a lawyer for a long time.

I regularly recommend to people who have equity but cannot afford their home in the long term to sell. My experience with the creditors' bar is that they will always take a settlement offer, no matter whether the account has been reduced to judgment and no matter how old the judgment is.

Last month a client, who was in foreclosure due to unpaid property taxes, found a buyer for her home. The house needed a lot of work, she was unable to keep up payments on the taxes, and decided to sell. She had about a half dozen judgment liens that resulted from old unpaid credit card accounts that remained outstanding. In order to complete the sale, I had to track them down and get them settled.

At least there was enough money from the equity in the property to pay them at closing. If this were a short sale, or if there wasn't enough equity to get them all paid and still leave her with some cash out of the deal, we probably wouldn't have bothered. Then my strategy for her would have been to keep her in the home as long as possible and eventually move when the time came.

Four out of her six unpaid liens were simple to deal with. In addition to getting the lien information from the closing attorney's title search, the original case information is usually available on our court website. I put my client's name into the search field and found the cases, including the names of the lawyers who initiated each suit against her. I just had to call them up and make settlement offers. We averaged just about 50% overall on those. The lesson here is it is always worth trying to get a discount so that the homeowner can keep as much of the cash out of the closing as possible.

I'm still tracking down the other two liens. Most of the cases against my client were brought by third party "debt buyers,", like the ones described elsewhere in this book. The problem here is that the law firms that get the judgments don't often continue to service the judgments, especially five or more years after the judgment enters, which was the case with my client. I know with a little more effort I'll find the companies currently handling the judgments and get them settled and paid. But in the meantime, we have to set aside the full amount of the judgment for these two liens in order to close, and my client won't get anything that is left over until we know what these companies will accept in settlement.

She had another creditor who obtained a judgment but had not filed a judgment lien. We still settled that one out because I feared that if we did not, and sold the house, the creditor's attorney would discover my client disposed of her only asset and it would cause a major problem later. It hurt because it was the highest balance of any of her outstanding accounts, but the closing attorney and I decided it was the right thing to do.

We also discovered that two judgments were taken against her on the same overdue account. It took me a little while to figure that out, then to disentangle them from each other, then get the firm who first got judgment to tell the second firm who got judgment that it was paid, so the second firm could provide a lien release. Don't try this at home, folks.

10. A Few Tips

Annie Hall said, "Eighty percent of life is just showing up," and I certainly don't dispute that. It makes sense in a number of ways and it's a great tip especially when you are facing registered letters and being served papers by state marshals.

Funny thing about showing up – things happen. Funny thing about not showing up – bad stuff happens. A friend of mine once put it this way: if you do something, something happens. If you do nothing, nothing happens. But let me clarify, when it comes to court, nothing *good* happens when you do nothing.

So the single most important thing I can, and do, tell anyone facing foreclosure, or small claims court, or wage garnishment, or anything requiring action in a court of law, is *Show up*.

When it comes to court actions, what many, many people don't get is this: you, and at some point, hopefully your attorney are the only people in the process there to protect your rights. That you have many rights in any action is indisputable, it's just that the judge and opposing party have no reason to protect them for you.

If you don't show up the process becomes this: "How quickly can we clear the case?" Let's say it's a foreclosure. The bank's law firm wants it off their growing pile of cases as soon as possible for profit's sake; the judge and clerk want the docket sheet cleared as they are graded on efficiency; the bank wants someone, anyone, paying something, as soon as possible.

So here's what happens when you don't show up and you leave your matter entirely in the hands of the bank's attorney and the court: they move as quickly and efficiently as possible to clear the case off the court's docket. In a foreclosure, this means your time is soon up.

The only way to stop this is to show up. It's that simple.

The neat thing about showing up, by the way, is it works at almost any point in the process. It's almost never too late. The sooner you do, though, the more options you have.

This reminds me of something a friend always says to me when I tend to repeat stories: *"This is where I came in."* It's kind of our cue to change subjects, or to do something different.

It's a phrase from the days when movie theaters ran features on a continuous loop. Walk in for a 4:15 show at 5:15, watch the last 45 minutes or so, then stay as the movie starts again. Bang, right back into it, you stay until you're caught up, you leave ... where you came in.

This was such a thing that some movies - *Psycho*, in particular - used it as a marketing tool. "Absolutely No One Admitted After The Start!"

Today, there are so many ads and trailers before every movie that I, at least, need to be reminded what film I'm there to see by the time the theater finally goes dark. Even without all that, in this day of spoiler alerts, it would never work without some form of violence.

Also - can you imagine seeing *Pulp Fiction* this way? Impossible to follow, I'm willing to bet.

Which is exactly what showing up in court after the case starts is: tough to catch up. If they still let you in, because a lot of court actions come with the Alfred Hitchcock admonition, "No one ... but no one" can participate after certain court proceedings start. But there's always a chance, usually at least one option left.

In court, particularly in foreclosure proceedings, we have to show up on time, sit through the ads and the coming attractions and go step by step, on time, from there. The point of no return in a foreclosure, however, is anytime after the credits start to roll. The court rarely hits rewind or lets you back in to watch from the start. Show up at any point before then and there's probably still a chance. Assume it's worth a try.

§

I know someone who zipped through law school finals (usually the one and only grade for a class, so, hey, no pressure) by creating flow charts. Elaborate charts that, if used properly, would lead to a well-organized, rational, factually-based answer. The trick for him – and anyone using it in lieu of an outline – was to properly identify the issue. Miss the issue and the flow chart was useless. Hit the issue, sit back and fill in the blanks.

Most options are, of course, at the beginning. Start with the basic issue(s) and it begins to narrow down, and down, and down to the logical end point – a logical, legally supportable result.

I thought of this when I was giving a short talk at the Connecticut Bar Association about foreclosure defense. I was talking about the process – always the process – and it always came back to options. As in, what options are available to the client at what point in the process.

Like my friend's flow charts, the options are very much front-loaded. The issue is not in doubt, but the way to a good result for the client is certainly not a straight line.

After I fielded a few questions it became clear, quickly, that my colleagues and I are seeing clients at the mid- to late stages of the process . . . the place where, under the flow chart scenario, the options narrow.

This is disturbing because this isn't a legal exercise, it's peoples' lives. It's their homes. It's even more disturbing if the reason for this is because people who are going through foreclosure don't think they have options . . . and by the time they realize they do, or reach out to find out, those options have been significantly reduced.

Either way, homeowners facing foreclosure have a textbook worth of options at the start of the process, and need to take advantage before they disappear.

§

When it came out in the theater, I took a group of clients to see *The Big Short*. It's a great movie, both fun and infuriating. It's about how we got into this mess – the burst of the bubble, the great recession, housing crisis, ongoing foreclosures. I wanted my clients to see how it all happened. It was a sobering overview of the last few years.

That year promised to be a year of movies about the financial crisis, recession, and aftermath and I've recently had a chance to see one of the latest, *99 Homes*. Okay, actually, I saw *Money Monster* first, but that's so far out of the realm of reality as to be meaningless (unless you believe that Julia Roberts and George Clooney solving a pending financial disaster/scam in a few hours has some real-world application).

99 Homes, on the other hand, was a kick in the stomach. It was visceral, it was brutal. It began with a court hearing in Orlando, Florida. A twenty-second hearing in which a character is told the paperwork is in order and he will be evicted by the bank in the morning. The eviction scene was tense and just heart-ripping. It was hard to watch. Realistic. Too realistic.

Something hit me in the brief moments before that scene, though. It was quick and it could certainly have been overlooked in what followed, except that it is repeated later in the movie, a few times actually, albeit in different forms: a shot of the homeowner at a kitchen table buried in paperwork. He's frantically burrowing through it while calling attorneys on his cell phone the night before his eviction. It becomes clear that our protagonist ignored what looks like at least dozens of notices from the bank, court, and the sheriff's office.

Later, as the movie takes some dark turns and heads toward the "99" homes of the title, it's obvious that most of the people Michael Shannon's (great in this, as in almost everything else) character is evicting have done exactly the same thing: they've ignored notices, even ones stuck on their front doors by Day-Glo red tape.

It's a theme I've explored more than a few times in my blog and when I speak in public and really thought I had a handle on. But seeing it on screen was hard. There's a natural reaction to wanting bad news to go away without having to do anything. There's the depression that hits, the "Nah, this isn't really happening" denial and most of the steps normally associated with the grieving process.

Except here, as so vividly shown in the film, there is no acceptance, just sheriffs and a bank representative at the door to wrest the home away. We don't see a resolution or happy ending. It isn't neatly wrapped up by the end. It's a lot like life.

You only see banks and happy endings together in TV commercials.

§

Who knew Disney would put out a move about foreclosure: *Mary Poppins Returns*.

You read that correctly, the new Mary Poppins movie centers around the Banks family (I just saw the irony in their name) struggling to keep their home. Good ol' Disney has added foreclosure to its repertoire of tragic plot lines.

Of course the foreclosure in Mary Poppins Returns is unrealistic and much more nightmarish compared to how foreclosure actually works here, in the U.S. and in Connecticut.

The themes were similar, and they got one right, but most of them wrong.

They nailed the main theme: when a crisis hits and causes financial struggle, usually a household can survive that; it's when a SECOND crisis hits when the mortgage goes unpaid. The first crisis in the movie was the Great Depression of the 1930's. I won't give away what the second crisis was, but any fans of Disney can take a wild guess...

You do get notice of foreclosure and a relatively reasonable amount of time in my state to work things out with your bank. The movie gave the impression you have little to no time to work out a solution with the bank or find a solution that is better suited for your household. You don't get a notice nailed to your door with only five days to pay up or move out like the Banks family did. We even have a mediation program that slows the whole process down.

The Banks family also only focused on one possible way to solve their problem. You might think you have only one option too, but time and again my meetings with homeowners end with us making a list of solutions to getting out of foreclosure.

The bad guy in the movie was the head of the bank: he sabotaged the family's attempt to solve the foreclosure, he was eager to foreclose not only on their home but multiple others, even setting quotas of foreclosures for the bank's attorneys to fulfill. He went so far as to say he wanted THEIR home. This is how most homeowners in the U.S. feel who are in foreclosure—as I have said before, it feels personal but it really isn't. No, your bank doesn't want your house, but despite that I can't explain the zeal with which they move to foreclose.

And you have a lot of stuff; years worth of stuff to sort through; so moving is going to be tedious, take you weeks or months, and be very emotional and difficult. The movie got this totally wrong with how it portrayed the Banks family's resignation and bright attitude about leaving their longtime home; it was – like Mary Poppins' shenanigans—unrealistic, without the feel-good magic.

Last but not least, the family had no lawyer. This allowed the head of the bank to conceal valuable information from the family, to deny them any options other than full payment. They had no one to speak for them, to keep an eye out for other ways to solve the problem or to negotiate a payment plan.

I see this a lot—a homeowner will just take a bank's word for it when they are told what their options are or what they have to do and by when. This usually ends up with a shorter timeframe for leaving the house- and when you're facing a deadline, five months can feel like five days, the amount of time the Banks family had to pay up or else. The movie got that right—without help, you're on your own, scrambling for a solution while fighting the clock.

I guess all the exaggeration makes for better on-screen drama. But who needs that in real life?

§

I have a friend who is a huge baseball fan. He's deep into baseball history, is still mad at Hollywood for changing the ending of *The Natural*, and makes a good case that Jim Bouton's *Ball Four* is one of the top five non-fiction baseball books of all time. He makes an even stronger case that *Ball Four* is one of the best business books ever.

This favorite story from the book seems particularly relevant to my practice and clients. It goes like this:

Ball Four takes place over the course of the one and only year of the 1969 Seattle Pilots – one of the most forlorn major league baseball teams of all time.

Late in the season the Pilots trade one of their very few legitimate major leaguers, Tommy Davis, to the Houston Astros.

Davis is thrilled to leave the gloom of last place and the almost daily rain delays of the even gloomier Sick's Stadium for The Eighth Wonder of the World (the Astrodome) and a shot at the pennant.

A few weeks into his Astros' experience Davis is so outwardly happy one of his new teammates, the intellectual flake and third baseman Doug Rader, can't stand it any longer and asks him why.

Tommy goes off on a litany of wonderful things that have happened since he stepped off the plane from Seattle to be met by the Houston General Manager and a limo: the Astros set him up in a fancy hotel until he could find a home, they flew his family down from Seattle first class, took his wife out to explore neighborhoods and school systems, are paying for meals and expenses while they're waiting to find a house, have a moving company packing up their Seattle home and bringing everything down all expenses paid, and a whole lot more. The Astros have, in fact, treated Davis so well he feels so indebted to them that he tells Rader he never wants to leave.

To which Doug Rader shakes his head slowly, puts a hand on Davis' shoulder and says, "They had to do all that, Tommy, it's in your contract."

We forget about The Contract. By missing payments, all of my clients have violated their contracts, the document they signed off on promising what they would do, what they would pay, then they come to me long after because they have been trying to work things out with the bank, or collection company, or some other institution, either because they were being told what they wanted to hear, or they believed they couldn't afford an attorney, or both. They felt obligated to work it out on their own because, like Tommy Davis, they think the bank is going out of its way to help them when, in fact, the bank is doing exactly what is required of it – and no more – under the terms of the contract. The contract actually anticipates that you will breach, and that is where the bank gets to start doing all kinds of things to you. It doesn't even have to help you, that's not in the contract.

Bank representatives can sound so helpful, leading to a false but understandable sense of "gratitude" during a time of great stress. It's fine to try to "work it out with the bank," of course, but it's important to do so from a position of knowledge. You need to talk to someone who knows what is really going on.

My friend tells me that as far as knowing what is going on and understanding The Contract, I have a very high WAR – Wins Above Replacement. Now I just need someone to explain that to me.

11. Self Help

"There's always free cheddar in the mousetrap, baby…"

That's a line from a Tom Waits song called, fittingly enough, *God's Away on Business*.

I help people involved in really scary personal financial debacles – it doesn't get much worse than having someone trying to take your house … unless you've had your identity stolen, or …

I deal in issues that became crises shortly after the Recession began and are still going strong.

People being people, no crisis has ever come and gone without someone figuring out how to gain from the misery. As far back as the Black Plague, charlatans masqueraded as doctors and roamed the streets peddling cures, charging exorbitant fees from increasingly desperate survivors.

It's a given that whenever and wherever there's a crisis there are the people who try to fix it, people who flee, people who suffer, and people who find a way to make easy money.

The Recession was not pretty, its effects have been lingering even though it was declared officially over. It led to the spate of foreclosures clogging courts across the U.S. that, per the latest reports, haven't peaked yet. Depending on when you think the "downturn" started, that's at least ten years of misery for a significant percentage of homeowners.

These ten years also happened to have coincided with the most prolific, almost instantaneous, exchange of information in human history. It's no surprise that the Internet is alive with conspiracy theories– conspiracies involving banks, mortgage lenders, government entities, brokerage firms, real estate investment companies, hedge funds, foreclosure law firms, and a host more. Also no surprise then that when it comes to foreclosures, the Internet is teeming with free advice, theories, legal forms, briefs, motions and magic potions to combat those conspirators.

As is the case with a lot of the Internet, the advice starts out free, little bits of "if you do this" and "do that" you might "end up with this." Just enough free advice to get you started while jamming the courts with unsupported pleadings.

Somewhere along the road, of course, maybe just to cover the cost of maintaining such a helpful site, there's a charge. That place usually occurs at a key junction of the case. The charges will not, of course, stop there. Think a smart phone/tablet game app – if you want to win you have to start racking up in-app purchases.

Here are a few more stories about people feasting off crises.

§

A friend of mine was talking to a woman last year, a potential foreclosure client, who had inherited a house about three months before the bank – one of the biggies – foreclosed.

She had already poured through the Internet reading and watching everything pertaining to foreclosure and the Recession. She was convinced, probably rightfully so, that her relative had been the victim of predatory lending and dove headlong into the whole sub-prime, securitized loan morass.

She was trying to decide between hiring a "regular" Connecticut foreclosure attorney and "fight it the normal way" or getting an out-of-state "sub-prime, securitized loan expert attorney" with affiliated lawyers in Connecticut and a proven track record.

She explained that the lawyer and his firm – out of Florida– were out to attack the securitization process, the mortgage note and what sounded like all the banking injustices of the last twenty something years. It was if the firm was infused with the quiet outrage of Matt Damon's narration in *Inside Job* while having the knowledge and legal "chops" to do something about it. But you know, if it is on the Internet, it must be true.

Great. Go get 'em. Win one for all the little guys.

Then my friend showed me the Florida firm's contract, all seven single-spaced pages. Aside the sizable up-front retainer and required 12-month payment plan – a full $500 more per month than the mortgage – and the expenses, and a contingency fee of 25% of damages or modification, and ten other problems I had with the thing, one item stood out head and shoulders above the rest:

Failure to pay the firm will lead to an "Attorney's Lien" being placed on the property. . . and any other property the client owns. Against their own client, the client in foreclosure, the client they have promised to help who has just gone through years of great financial stress.

Just to be clear, we're not talking regular Connecticut "let's-work-within-the system-and-achieve-something-that-helps-everyone" fees, we're talking "let's-take-on-the-system-and-make-the-banks-pay-while-I-get-rich" fees. In this case $27,500 the first year, plus expenses.

I would describe that with one of my favorite expressions: "Out of the frying pan, into the fire." But it was on the Internet, so it must be true.

Remember Bullwinkle, lead character of probably one of the best cartoons of all time? Subversive is a pretty apt description of the show in those way-way-way back pre-cable days. One of Bullwinkle Moose's favorite expressions is: "*If it's in the newspaper, it must be true,*" (try to hear his voice when you read that).

It was satirical then and it's satirical now: substitute the word Internet for the word newspaper and "If it's on the Internet, it must be true," would be Bullwinkle's new catchphrase. Most people would laugh, shake their heads and agree – even the ones who repost photos of Obama and the aliens from Roswell drinking beer on Facebook.

That doesn't stop anyone from finding and believing exactly what they want to find, and believe, online. This seems to particularly apply to legal matters. Let's face it, there have been some insane court decisions over the past few hundred years, there's bound to be one floating around out there for any "no hope" scenario.

There have been a few real outliers when it comes to foreclosures – homeowners who, through a long series of tortuous litigation (is that redundant?), end up with a "free house." In the time it took to get the free house there were probably thousands of modifications, negotiated short sales, all manner of not-so-horrible outcomes for other homeowners. Yet the once-in-a-lifetime, all the planets perfectly aligned, outcome hits the Internet with all the subtlety of a Floyd Mayweather news conference.

This is the bane of my lawyerly existence. Unlike Bullwinkle's newspapers, news of "A Resounding Victory for Homeowners" doesn't stay in the Business section or end up on the bottom of a bird cage – it spreads like wildfire and the more it spreads the more the magic of SEO kicks in and the higher it pops up in searches and the more people believe they can achieve the same result. But "for a price, Ugarte, for a price." (This time it's Humphrey Bogart's voice.)

The cycle is fed by homeowners under threat of foreclosure searching the Net for help tempted by dozens and dozens of "*I got my home for free*," "*I got my client a house for free*," "*you can get your house for free*," articles, blog posts, outright solicitations. So many that they think it must be true.

Case in point, a large foreclosure firm filed suit against a homeowner in southeastern Connecticut. The homeowner skipped filing a response in the state court and went straight to Federal District Court with a complaint against his bank that the court generously referred to as "Somewhat repetitive, verbose, and dense."

The homeowner's complaint was straight off the web and it attacked the forest while forgoing the trees. The District Court was not unsympathetic to some piece of the argument, tried several times to direct the homeowner toward something legally solid (the court, in fact, did everything except use highlighter over the relevant passages). But he failed to take the hint, missing the golden opportunities offered by the court. The foreclosure firm made a half dozen procedural errors in its pursuit of the state foreclosure action but the homeowner – guided by the web-based conspiracy crowd – ignored those less glamorous arguments in his attempt to slay the giant.

After a long and tortuous process, the homeowner lost and the foreclosure firm touted it as a notable, precedent-setting win on various industry web sites. Every side is entitled to their own illusions.

The thing is, maybe there was (and is) a conspiracy or three. Certainly a lot of bad things happened to take down the economy. None of that matters; the time and the place to blow the lid off it is not while you are in the thick of the foreclosure process yourself. You need all your energy to work to keep your home or stay in it as long as possible while you rearrange your life.

These websites and self-help programs feed off of a homeowner's stress and confusion. They do not offer solutions based on realistic outcomes for actual homeowners. It's just modern snake oil.

Fast forward again and we see what charlatans emerge with the mortgage crisis. With the power of computers and the Internet, scammers could thrive, reach more people and make more profit. Everything else we enjoy about the Information Age has also been used by the scammers to profit by disseminating clouds of bad information that just buries the good.

I see it every day. I warn people and spend an inordinate amount of time debunking newly minted myths. My assistant recently forwarded me an article about a scam in Detroit that's as audacious as it is heartbreaking: getting people to lease-to-own abandoned homes, fix them up, pay for years under written agreements to purchase, only to find out that the individual they signed a lease with and who they thought owned the property has never paid the real estate taxes. Or the mortgages. Or anything. The real estate management company, the leasing company, the company holding the mortgages, and the financing company all had slightly different roles and were completely, totally removed from any responsibility under those contracts.

This path to homeownership looked spectacular on paper, or at least it did on the website. The scammers promised the city it could clean up Detroit's blighted neighborhoods, Detroit funded the company with public pension funds, but lost them. It promised citizens of Detroit a home, instead it delivered foreclosure notices.

The foreclosure crisis is not over and the charlatans are still out there. Every time someone runs a Google search for "foreclosure defense," or "debt consolidation," or "credit card help," you'll see my site duking it out for homeowners' attention with the guys selling snake oil.

§

An attorney and a real estate guy were arrested in Connecticut for allegedly running a scam on people facing foreclosure who wanted a way out of their mortgages and their homes.

According to the Connecticut Law Journal *"[They] would offer to purchase [homes of distressed borrowers] and pay off the mortgages. The distressed homeowners agreed to sign various documents, including quitclaim deeds, indemnification agreements, management agreements and third-party authorization letters that [they] presented to them with the promise that they would be able to walk away from their homes debt-free."*

The lawyer then told the homeowners they could ignore any future communications from their own banks, they were all set, they could move out and never worry about anything again – court notices, collection calls, credit scores. The common refrain of the American lawyer: "Don't worry."

After the homeowners moved out, the alleged scammers then rented out the homes and pocketed the rent. No money was ever forwarded to either the real owners or the banks. It's assumed that this went on until the banks ultimately foreclosed and the renters received eviction notices.

This was my state's version of the Detroit scam. Distressed homeowners are just that. Aside from serious health issues there are few things more stressful than facing losing one's home. Distressed homeowners are targets for the smart but unscrupulous. These predators invented fantastical solutions that sounded dead-on doable to desperate people.

Here's the thing, and it's simple - if someone says they'll handle everything, deal with the bank for you, take all the stress off, allow you to ignore future notices and all those pesky court dates, they are ripping you off.

Get a lawyer, go to court, handle it directly, there is no magic to it. Real Estate Maven, Lawyer, Doctor, your favorite brother-in-law, anyone who tells you they have the solution and you can ignore everything is not there to help.

Deal with these types of people and you'll end up like Flounder from *Animal House*. Remember, he loans the guys his brother's car for the infamous road trip and it comes back so trashed it's unrecognizable. The response from Otter? To paraphrase, "Face it, you screwed up, you trusted us."

§

You may remember this from 2018, the former *Cosby Show* actor Geoffrey Owens was "outed" by a shopper armed with an iPhone when she ran across him working at a Trader Joe's. It was another example of debt shaming: the actor had lost his steady income source, residuals from *The Cosby Show*, that went away when the show was pulled from syndication because of the sexual abuse charges leveled at Bill Cosby.

Just like many of my clients, an unexpected change in income had a disastrous effect.

Though, it really needs to be noted, when confronted, Owens admitted that he really loved working at Trader Joe's.

The same actor had just landed a small role as the type of lawyer we hardly see on TV (but he and *Better Call Saul*'s Jimmy McGill could definitely swap stories. He was cast as Gerald Watkins Mayfield in HBO's *Divorce*.

Divorce is the story of a successful business woman, Frances (Sarah Jessica Parker) and her not quite as successful husband, Robert (Thomas Hayden Church) living in Hastings-on-Hudson NY, a pretty, upscale town on the Hudson River an hour or so north of New York City. The town, by the way, is pretty much a character.

Obviously, they have marital problems. They go through all the motions of therapy and reconciliation and mediation, it's clear six shows or so in that they need to divorce and it's going to get ugly.

They need lawyers. Robert is not the type to ask around or spend time on Google, or, indeed, doing anything proactive. Eventually, though, a friend introduces him to a relative who's an attorney right in town and who "does everything." That would be Gerald Watkins Mayfield and he pushes all of my buttons about how not to practice law.

He works out of his garage and his wife pops in every few minutes to remind him to "Watch the oven, dinner's in," but, all in all, it's pretty charming. Until he starts talking. Then it's funny but chilling - if you're a lawyer.

The scene (easily the funniest in the show, period):

"So, you do mostly divorces?"

"Nope, mostly wills, trusts, estates."

"You do some divorces?"

"You know what, Robert? Basically, it's all law."

That's it, in a nutshell, perfectly put by a great character. "*Basically, it's all law.*"

It's not, of course, but clients still buy into it. As Robert does. Disastrously. I'll leave it to you to watch the show to see just how disastrous it is.

For now, though, just understand that if you need a divorce attorney, hire a firm that does *family law;* need an estate plan? Hire an estate planning firm; are facing a foreclosure? Retain someone who does exactly that most of her working day.

12. Rights and Responsibilities

A lot of people I talk to have what they believe are legitimate questions about help if you fall behind on your mortgage. Isn't there some program for me? I heard the President wants to help people in my situation. Where is my bailout? Unfortunately, the questions are simply a sad reflection of how the middle-class homeowner is treated in this country. The people who ask these questions are usually the ones in foreclosure, or who are not yet in foreclosure but who are months and months behind in their mortgage payments, and they truly believe there is a "program" for them out there.

I don't blame them. There seems to be a program for every other segment of society—if you can't buy food there's food stamps; if you can't afford rent there's Section 8 housing vouchers; if you are disabled there's Social Security Disability insurance programs; if you're a corporation that employs lots of people there are tax breaks, and government loans to keep you afloat (aka "bailouts").

So what is there for the middle class?

"Isn't there some kind of program that I qualify for, after all, I paid on this mortgage for 10 years without missing a single payment, I even paid early, but now I've lost all my overtime and my wife is going to be out of work for 8 weeks recovering from a hysterectomy and she doesn't have any disability insurance and probably won't be able to go back to work as a CNA after because her back is bad from all the lifting that job requires. There must be some help for me out there."

Sorry, sir. There is not.

Why not?

There just isn't.

But how can that be?

My response, because I really don't know how to explain it, and this really does make sense if you think about it, is a quote from an obscure Amendment to the Constitution:

"Because you are not required to quarter soldiers in your home."

Huh?

Yes, right after the right to bear arms (the Second Amendment- not that you needed reminding) and the right against unlawful searches and seizures (the Fourth Amendment – again, we all know that one), is the Third Amendment:

"No soldier shall, in time of peace be quartered in any house, without the consent of the Owner, nor in time of war, but in a manner to be prescribed by law."

Again, I usually get, "Um, huh?" And I explain it thus:

In Colonial times, citizens were required to put English soldiers up in their homes at the homeowners' expense. Now these were not homeowners who received a paycheck direct deposited into their bank accounts every other Friday, and their homes did not have 4 bedrooms, 3 ½ bathrooms with granite countertops in their kitchens and your choice of several grocery stores within a five-mile radius. There were probably four walls, but likely only one bed for everyone, including the dog, one fireplace, and some kind of outhouse in the back yard. Adding another body to that kind of home was a real hardship for the Colonial family. And then he had to be fed, and the woman of the house likely had to launder his clothes and shine his boots and mend his socks. Oh yeah, and they all wore powdered wigs back then, so there was that to worry about too, on top of her own husband's and children's upkeep…

I explain that if we were still required to quarter soldiers in our homes – if we had to house and feed and do laundry for members of the military for any amount of time-- there would probably be a government subsidy for us. But we get to shut our doors (Fourth Amendment) against the eyes of the government. We don't have to share our resources with anyone else beyond paying our taxes, and so there is no help for us.

That may seem like a bit of a stretch. But take the First Amendment's protection of free speech and look how broadly it is now interpreted.

Same with the Second Amendment, which was designed to permit local militia to arm themselves, but now allows citizens (and local police) to become mini armies of their own.

And the Fourth Amendment, the way it has been expanded to encompass the entire concept of privacy.

Why not interpret the freedom from the requirement to house soldiers as a way to explain why Americans get no housing subsidy if they are "wealthy" enough to be able to obtain a mortgage? I have no problem imagining our country, where members of the military are held in extremely high regard, as one where local citizens are requested to house some soldiers at least from time to time, and are compensated for it. (I don't bother getting into the politics of how that would probably really help our nation's budget and help the modern middle-class homeowner if we implemented such a program.)

You get to shut your door against your government, I explain, but for that privilege you are on your own. There's no help for you.

Oh, ok, I get it.

The idea of being able to lock your doors and sit in front of the TV in your underwear and pick your nose in private and not have to answer to your government for it seems to make sense in this context.

But come on, there's no help? That doesn't seem fair.

My answer to that: It's not fair. It's Capitalism.

We are expected to lift ourselves up by our own bootstraps. You have the right to the *pursuit* of happiness, not a guarantee of it.

I'll say it again: not being able to pay your bills in a Capitalist economy is seen as a weakness. A character flaw. A basis to be able to pass judgment on our neighbors. It's survival of the most financially fit in this country.

189

What can the average homeowner do?

In my state, and in some others, there is a bailout, but it comes in an odd shape and form.

You just stop paying your mortgage.

Hold on—what?

That's right. Keep in mind-- this is not legal advice! But where I live, you can stop paying your mortgage and you can still be in your home up to two years later, sometimes more. If you're able to and you do it, you can and should save your mortgage payments, or as much of your mortgage payment as possible each month, and start a savings account.

Can't my bank get it? Can't they take it?

Here's where the Fourth Amendment comes into the conversation—maybe the bank can, but not without due process of law, which means obtaining a court order against you first. In my state, and in some others, the banks usually don't go that far.

In the meantime, I tell people to save as much money as possible— "In a coffee can, under your mattress, in a savings account, wherever, so long as you save and you don't use it for other things," is my mantra. I probably utter those words to clients at least twice a week.

Also, your lender usually has to give you notice that you are in default on your loan (90 or more days late), and give you time to "reinstate," pay off all the back payments and late fees. Many people cannot do that, that's over three months of mortgage payments at one time. But they get 45 days to try.

Then, where I live, after you're 90 days behind, and you've had 45 days to try to catch up, the bank will send the loan to a local attorney to start the foreclosure process. My favorite little law that I talked about earlier in this book, the Fair Debt Collection Practices Act, requires that these lawyers provide a notice that the homeowner has 30 days to dispute the debt. There's another month of delay. By the time this 30 days is up, you may be about six months behind or more.

The next step is for the local attorney to commence a lawsuit. My state has what is called "judicial foreclosure," that is, the court gets to decide whether the foreclosure occurs. That doesn't mean there's a lot of deliberation and individual examination of every case. That just means your bank can't foreclose without having taken the steps necessary to get a court to order it. If you're lucky to be in a state with judicial foreclosure like I am and like a handful of others, it can take many more months for the bank to get that court order.

During all this time your lender will not take any payments from you unless it is the exact amount to pay off all the months you are behind plus the late fees, interest, and if foreclosure has started, court costs and attorney's fees.

So, if the bank won't take your money, what do you do?

You save.

Let me back up a bit. People don't understand why the bank won't take their payments. A lawyer friend of mine thinks it's very suspicious, and phrases it this way: "It's a bank, their business is money. And they won't take money? That says to me they don't have the right to collect the money!" Then I have to listen to a half hour of even stranger conspiracy theories than the ones I already subscribe to… But he has a point. Banks that won't take money. Hmmm.

I blame the credit card companies for the widespread belief that your mortgage company can and should take any amount of payment at any time. This isn't such a leap. You have a credit card, you use the card, you can't pay off the entire balance at one time, so you pay the "minimum payment." You may even pay late and get charged a late fee.

But credit cards are "revolving" accounts, they have no end date, the balance just sits there, plus interest, until it gets paid. Mortgages are "installment" accounts. When you take out a mortgage, it's a contract, you are agreeing to make a certain number of monthly payments.

As I explained in an earlier chapter, most mortgages are thirty-year loans, so that's 360 monthly payments. They are laid out in a schedule from day one all the way to the end. And if you did not pay the payment for November, 2015, that payment will still need to be paid even if it is now months later. That is, if you missed the November, 2015 payment, but made a payment in December, 2015, the bank is going to credit the payment made in December toward the November payment. Many homeowners paying late don't pay the late fee, which was also due because your payment was due by about November 15.

If you made no payment in November and next paid in December, you were late for November, and the way some mortgages are structured, the $50 or $100 late fee is first taken out of the payment you made, and what is left is credited to the November payment. In that case, your November payment may have been short by the amount of the late fee.

You probably didn't know this and you probably also thought you were not late or behind by a month. Then when you pay again in January, a little of that payment goes toward finishing the November payment, a large part goes toward December's payment, and probably nothing toward the January payment (did you remember to add a late fee? Probably not.) So, you make a payment in February, and a little bit finishes what is still owed for December, and the rest goes to January, but most people who call me who are in this situation think they are paying on time. This can go on for months.

When we request a payment history and we see how the payments have been credited, finally the homeowner "gets it." But this is usually after the homeowner is served with foreclosure papers or notices. They are confused because they thought they were all caught up or maybe just one month behind, and by then they can't catch up all the way.

To an extent I blame the credit card industry for this. We have been trained by how we treat our credit card bills to pretty much pay what we can when we can so it's easy to think of your mortgage payment this way.

This is when many homeowners call me and within a few sentences I can tell that this is what happened- they missed or were very late on a payment somewhere, but they didn't realize it. It's not always their fault; many times homeowners will call their bank to say they can't make the whole payment or can't make it on time. The banks will usually try to put the homeowner into some kind of repayment plan, but I rarely see a bank explain this well enough, and I hardly ever see the homeowner understand the plan well enough. Before you know it you're more than 90 days behind and you can't pay three months all at once.

Now you'd think that even if you're more than 90 days behind and even if you can't pay three months of payments all at once that the bank would at least still *TAKE* your payments, no matter how big or small.

Enter my lawyer friend who thinks it's suspicious that they don't. Why send back a payment? Has anyone ever given you money and you voluntarily just give it back? Sometimes they take your payment—but unless you pay enough to stay less than 90 days behind (and you must send the payment before you go 90 days behind), they will just hold onto your money.

They put it in what are commonly called "suspense" accounts. Your money just sits there, not credited toward anything. You can keep paying but if the bank's policy is to hold your money in suspense, you aren't getting it back. You may think that you are doing good or avoiding trouble by sending your money in. But not necessarily.

Back to what you do if your bank won't accept your payments: you save.

If your payment is $1000 per month, and you can save that every month for a year, you have $12,000 saved up. Two years, $24,000. When I get the question, "Where is my bailout?" that is how I answer. If your bank won't take your payments, you save, and *THAT's* your bailout. So long as you are living in a house and you are not paying a mortgage, here's your chance to build up savings. When else in your life are you going to get free housing?

The key is being able to save, and not being tempted to pay down your credit cards, or get tires on the car, or get that dental work done you've been putting off. If you never fell behind, you would be sending that mortgage payment out the door every month. When clients indignantly say, "Well the bank wouldn't take our payments, so we paid off our cars!", I grab the large calculator that I keep on my conference room table and I do the math for them. I say, "OK, you haven't paid your mortgage in 13 months and you used to pay $1350 per month.

"That's $16,200 that you haven't spent in the last year." Then I do the math for my house. I tell them that my mortgage is $1600 per month and in the last 13 months I've spent $19,200 on my mortgage, and that's $19,200 that I could not and did not spend on other things. Technically, they are "up" $16,200, while the rest of us who are paying our mortgages are "down" by the amounts we have paid. Granted, we are not in foreclosure, but in this context, the homeowners sitting in my conference room are no victims.

This kind of exchange with clients really serves to get them to understand that they don't have the rights they think they have. They really don't have the expectation that they can live for free, that they don't have to pay for housing; they are just frustrated that the bank wouldn't work with them or help them when they needed help.

Do they have the right to feel that way? Of course. What kind of business model is it to have people in 30-year mortgages and provide no help at all during that 30 years even though it's statistically almost impossible to not suffer some kind of hardship that prevents you from being able to make every payment on time and in full for 360 consecutive months?

It's a terrible business model to treat homeowners like this. It's a stupid idea to default a homeowner if they are 90 days late and then stop taking any kind of payment. This doesn't make financial sense. Not in a post-2008 economy it doesn't.

Strange business practices on the part of the banks don't change the fact that today there are no real programs to help the homeowner who falls behind on his or her mortgage. At least no programs that don't require extensive review of the homeowner's financial documentation, and that are relatively ineffective.

Few homeowners live in states where the foreclosure process is slow enough that they can build up savings during the foreclosure process so at least they have some money to relocate and start over with.

There are no such programs in the pipeline either, especially now that the economy is perceived to be recovering, at least as of the date of this book's publication. No plans to start housing soldiers in your home either, but you can always write your Congressman and ask about that. You don't have to give me credit for the idea.

.

13. Expectations

Expectations are funny things – personal, largely unspoken, the basis for relationships, while probably one of the main reasons relationships fail.

In any relationship, the longer expectations are left unspoken, the more divergent they become until you get the situation below:

Foreclosure defense is rife with expectations, few of them grounded in what really occurs during the court process.

A few years ago, it was widely reported that up to 90% of people foreclosed on failed to show up at court. Period. Most of them no doubt expected that after missing mortgage payments, everything from there on out was inevitable – a quick look around the Internet easily reinforced that – so why add the stress of spending a day in court?

Many people going into foreclosure are angry – at themselves, their banks, mortgage brokers, investors that bought securitized mortgage instruments, Congress, Wall Street, and on and on – a quick look around the Internet easily reinforces this, too.

My job with both these categories – and all the ones in between, they tend to create some very interesting Venn Diagrams – is managing their expectations . . . no, that's wrong, my job is to set their expectations.

Simply: we are not going to court to roll up in a ball and acquiesce to everything the bank's lawyers toss at us; conversely, we are not going to court to right the wrongs of the Recession, undo the securitization of loans, return the financial world to the way it was in the good old days before . . .

I go to court to get a fair and equitable deal for you as best I can and take some stress out of your life.

That's it, anything else adds to the stress levels for all of us and can lead to perilous situations – and none of us have Bond's ability to escape time after time.

§

Talk about an unrealistic expectations.

Recently, news came down about a California Appeals Court decision where the court recognized that a mortgage company/bank suing for foreclosure could not produce the note and had used robo-signing on documents.

The court lambasted the bank and awarded considerable damages to the former homeowners - the house had been foreclosed on years earlier and sold.

The decision set off a barrage of Internet invective and off the wall speculation - i.e., use this case as a template, end up with a free house.

There's a lot wrong with this. First, maybe foremost, the decision in that case is based solely on the facts of that case. It's not your Starbucks card, it's not transferable. Second, that decision represents years of litigation and immense legal fees.

Then there's the free house. You know, scare off the mortgage company, make them so flummoxed by the legal brilliance you've taken from your careful reading of the California decision and stop them in their tracks.

Perfect, right? Well, perfect only if you and your family and your descendants want to live in the house forever. "But it needs a lot of work," a client will tell me. "A new roof, windows, furnace."

"Well, fight to keep that brokedown palace and that's what you're signing up for," I warn. I'm not sure they've thought of it that way before.

I've heard of someone in Central Connecticut who has, indeed, pulled this off. Has so intimidated the mortgage company and mortgage company lawyers that they dropped the case against him and walked away.

He still has his house. In name only. What he doesn't have and never will have is a clear title because technically the balance on the mortgage loan is still owed. He pays his property taxes but does not pay a mortgage. He cannot do any of the things people with clear title can do, like sell or refinance. Nothing. Unless, of course, he pays off the mortgage. But that wasn't the point.

The free house isn't really free. It's a ticking time bomb and it's an anchor ... unless you are willing to walk away from it. Then it's the neighbors' problem.

§

For about a week in the summer of 2016 I posted on Facebook about an upcoming race I had registered for and was training for: the Litchfield Hills Triathlon. I wasn't posting to help psych myself up for a rough, hot, intimidating race (okay, maybe a little), I was hoping to make a point. A strong point about a real problem my clients run into, especially when they are late becoming my client, that is they have gone it alone through a court hearing or two.

Let me back up: I had a running coach for this event. She outlined a comprehensive, step-by-step program to help me prepare for this race. I considered that vital - anyone who has ever driven around Litchfield, Connecticut would know why ... the word *HILLS* is in the name for a reason.

I followed the plan religiously ... until I didn't. Things got in the way. I am not a professional triathlete, I will never get any kind of sponsorship to pay for shoes, clothing, coaching, all that stuff. In short, I'm a business owner who runs (swims and bikes too, I suppose) to stay in shape and, most importantly, to stay mentally sharp.

So, things (life) got in the way of our perfect plan. A workout skipped, a mile or two skimped on, you know how it goes.

At no time during my training, however, did I ever run the risk of being kept from running the race. It wasn't like I had to check in on the morning of the race with my training program signed off on and in perfect order to race. No race clerk to verify my training and say, "It's all in order, go get in line, hand this to the starter and you're good to go."

It's certainly not like, in my case, there was someone to say, "Oh, hey, Sarah you missed a timed workout on June 8th, and this long run on the 20th ... sorry, you can't race. You're out ... it just wouldn't be fair to the racers who did the work."

No, that would have been ridiculous, anyone who pays a race fee and wants to abuse their body for a few hours can start the race. Anyone who has prepared at least somewhat has a chance to finish.

The "Sorry, you can't race scenario" does, however, appear throughout the foreclosure process. I give my clients a list of things they have to do. Same as my coach gave me. The difference is that if they skip an item or try to get by with a half measure, they stand a good chance of defaulting - they will get kicked out of the race.

My skipping workouts meant I just came in last (which I did). I still got the finisher's medal and a free t-shirt.

For the people who are debating getting an attorney because they think they've got a decent grasp on what should be on the list and how and when to get into the race ... well, usually I see those people at some point after it has started. While I can usually help, it's like running the race with a cramping hamstring - it can go a number of ways, only one is good. There's no participation medal in foreclosure. You either do the work and keep the house, or you're out. It's as simple as that.

§

To paraphrase one of the five worst people who ever lived, "When something really bad happens to one person, it's a tragedy; when it happens to a million, it's a statistic."

This is certainly true of foreclosures. At least today.

I bring this up because I am sometimes asked why I expend such time and energy defending foreclosure actions. I say sometimes because it's only occasionally verbally stated, usually it's expressed via "that look," a slight crinkling of the eyebrows, a thin, quick frown, maybe a brief tilt of the head when I say what I do.

Unless, of course, they have been through foreclosure themselves or had family or friends involved. Then I get a knowing nod, smile.

Why? Because years ago, before I graduated high school, foreclosures were something that happened to "other people" and in virtual secrecy. They were much, much rarer on the court calendars than they are today. And it probably took a lot more to get a case to court. Banks and mortgage companies were much more likely to be local - another word for approachable. You could talk to your banker, lender, face-to-face, work things out.

Foreclosures then were small tragedies that happened in the very occasional neighborhood.

The financial meltdown of 2007-8 changed that. In months, millions of homeowners were at risk and failing quickly. Very, very few local banks and lenders exist anymore, corporations and computers took over years ago. Out of necessity, the foreclosure process became industrialized.

The people in the long lines and crowded hallways in the courthouses have become statistics. In the eleven years since the meltdown the two largest foreclosure firms in the Greater Hartford area have filed over 80,000 foreclosure cases. And counting.

The great tragedy with that is individuals are lost. Completely. A file is a file is a statistic - win, lose, draw, but close the case.

So, when I get "that look" I try to bring it back to the first or second person, away from that horrible third person "them." The easiest, most effective way is to point out the effect of this crisis on neighborhoods - "Well, would you want a foreclosed house in your neighborhood? How about more than one?"

That takes it back to the first person pretty quickly. I can't enforce empathy, but I can provide it, though I wish I didn't have to.

14. Pack Your Bags

The routine in "short calendar," a weekly court session dedicated to arguing brief motions in cases in front of a judge, is that the judge usually takes the cases where attorneys have entered appearances first – ostensibly to try and curb expenses (who wants to pay a lawyer to sit in court all morning?). One day, the judge decided to take homeowners representing themselves first – the better so they don't miss work. A lot of homeowners representing themselves don't show up, but they did that day. I probably let out an audible sigh, but relaxed when I thought about all the times my cases were heard early.

I sat through foreclosure story after foreclosure story listening to a lot of solid explanations why homes shouldn't be foreclosed on.

One man explained he fell behind after his house sustained storm damage. His insurance company assured him he would be reimbursed in full for the repairs. Two checks came and he paid the contractors but then, for some reason, the bank held the last $19,000 check.

He is in the beginning of a foreclosure while still trying to work things out with the bank. That's it, he, by himself, is working with his bank to get money released and start to "take care of the mess."

The judge set a date and if the homeowner didn't resolve the problem in time the bank would own his house. The poor guy had the attitude of someone who just can't believe that the problem won't get resolved, that the bank won't do the right thing. Eventually.

Other families came before the judge with different stories based on the same theme – the bank made them a promise and they'll be following up … soon.

All of them were given foreclosure dates.

The general rule is once you don't feel your bank is helping you or listening to you, you need to stop seeking help and advice from the bank. If you were arrested, would you ask the cops for help? I think we have been trained from all the law shows on TV to know there's an adversarial relationship between the police and someone who has been arrested (even if the person is innocent). What TV hasn't taught us – because how un-sexy would a show about foreclosure court be – is that the banks and mortgage lenders are the cops and homeowners have the right to remain silent and have the right to seek the advice of an attorney. People who are arrested know that without an attorney they are likely to lose some liberties- likely to spend time in jail. People in foreclosure are also at risk of losing similar liberties- like the right to own their homes- if they don't seek out the advice of an attorney.

§

In my state, judges are typically assigned types of dockets for at least one year—some judges stay in their assignments for more than one year, but typically every September there is a shake up and a judge who last month was hearing divorces is now hearing foreclosures, for example.

Then there are days when judges are out sick or on vacation. This story is about one of those days.

The substitute judge assigned to the foreclosure hearings on that gloomy Monday was a retired judge, one whom I'd argued in front of many times before the judge's retirement. I had known this judge to be reasonable and generally sympathetic to my clients. I liked how this judge tended to lob me softballs from the bench, such as, "Now counselor, can you explain to me again how the other party harmed your client?" And I would get to tell my client's story, with detail of just exactly how he or she was wronged and just which parts of what laws the other guy violated, to a courtroom full of people. That to me was a good judge.

I had been in front of this judge at least once since retirement and that didn't go well. No softballs, didn't seem to have read any of the file or at least the motions that were on the calendar that day in advance, and decided to give a ruling, very adverse to my client, from the bench anyways. Hmmm. That was too bad.

Fast forward and here I am again in a courtroom where this judge is making rulings on foreclosure cases. Up at the table is a middle-aged man about to have a deadline set for him to pay all his back mortgage payments (a virtually impossible task for the average American worker) or else the bank would own his house.

He stated what he did for a living and it sounded to me he was a good candidate to modify his mortgage. He stated that he wanted to work with the bank on a modified payment (a very common solution when you can't make up all your past due mortgage payments in one lump), but that due to all the double shifts he was working, he didn't have time to get all the extensive paperwork together to complete an application for a modified mortgage.

While the judge extended by a month the date that would normally be given out as a deadline for him to make the payments or modify his mortgage, the order also included an admonition: "Sir, you better pack your bags."

I was appalled.

The order essentially gave him 8 weeks to accomplish an excruciating task or he would no longer own his home. And it didn't even appear the judge was listening- he had other options than to "pack his bags" but the judge didn't give any indication of hope at all.

First, it was clear this guy could have been a viable candidate to get back on track if he could modify his mortgage. He had a good job—that is really the only thing needed so long as you earn enough so that a recalculation of your total debt, even with back payments added onto the end of the loan or with an adjustment of the interest rate (both common methods to modify mortgages) would still result in an affordable monthly payment based on that income.

Second, he stated he had been working so hard that he wasn't able to jump through the hoops needed to do the necessary paperwork. This is not a frivolous claim—the paperwork required to apply to modify a mortgage can be extensive, complicated, and filled with tricks and traps. I have had applications rejected because one little box wasn't checked off, or an obscure, practically hidden request for a homeowner to identify the number of people in the household was not completed.

Mortgage lenders or the underwriters they assign to review modification applications are also not very good at telling you what they are looking for. In one case, the lender kept asking the client to submit a tax form called a 4506-t. We had submitted several and although the forms have an expiration date, the requests for the form were renewed several times before the client's form expired.

Finally, I took a close look at the form we kept resubmitting— we had mistakenly omitted one digit of the client's Social Security number on the form. Not a minor error, I admit, but the lender never indicated *why* we had to keep resubmitting the form; if I hadn't discovered the error the client may have been denied a modification and lost their home and we may not have ever known why.

So maybe it's just me, but when a judge hears that a homeowner is working double shifts, and wants to modify a mortgage, I'd like to think the judge would recognize that this case could be resolved and the home saved and provide the homeowner a little guidance on how to go about that despite his limited time and resources to help himself.

"Pack your bags" didn't seem particularly constructive in that regard, and in fact to me was blatantly misleading. Any homeowner told this by a judge would think he had no chance at saving his home.

One thing led to another and this client came to see me. You can probably guess where this is going: in less than 6 weeks (rocket fast in the mortgage modification process) the client was on track and making "trial" payments toward his mortgage. Within three months we were back in court on the *bank's* request to vacate that order of foreclosure, and the case was dropped.

The client wanted to be there the day the order was vacated. He was hoping we'd get the same judge who issued the foreclosure order and told him to pack. I wanted that judge to be there too. But the regularly assigned judge was in court that day and so that substitute judge did not have to answer to this homeowner.

I still wonder whether I would have reminded the judge that this was the homeowner who, in the judge's eyes, had no hope of saving his home, and whether I would have said something like "Look at him now!" It haunts me how many other homeowners have been told similar things by so many other judges around the state (or the country). For now, I'll have to be satisfied that I released one from the snare of the judge's ignorance.

In all fairness (though I say that with a certain tone), the role of the judge is not to advocate for any of the parties before the court. But I'd like to think that judges can (and some do) see what is going on, especially when people represent themselves, and act in a way for the greater good.

Figuring out a way to lead this homeowner to the resources, and then giving him the time to meaningfully go through the mortgage modification application process, could be one way to serve the public good. After all, banks don't want more foreclosed homes in their inventories and our communities are not served when hardworking (or disabled, or grieving, or unemployed) homeowners are displaced because they couldn't solve their foreclosure problems within the deadlines set by a court.

Would it be advocating for a homeowner to provide the space for him to save his home? Was his mortgage company (in this case, one of the largest in the land) going to go broke if it didn't foreclose on his house and put it into its ever-growing inventory of empty homes?

A little creativity to get to the right result is all I ask for.

On behalf of my client to the judge who issued his foreclosure judgment, if you're listening: He saved his house when you told him he could not. It was possible but you didn't know enough, subbing for another judge, or you knew enough but didn't want to be bothered, to know that this homeowner could have saved his home. You of all people should not be misleading homeowners. Please don't do it again.

§

Lawyers are heavily regulated. I know it may not seem that way to the public, but we have to follow a lot of rules. Many of those rules are designed to protect the public. "Ambulance chasing" has been, well, chased off for the most part, and lawyers' contacts with potential clients are heavily regulated.

For example, if I learn of a homeowner who might need help fending off a foreclosure, I can't call that homeowner (or have anyone else call them for me); and if I choose to contact that person via letter, I have to stamp ADVERTISING MATERIAL in big red letters on the envelope and the letter. That's because an average member of the public might think they HAVE to respond to a letter they receive from a lawyer, but this "warning" makes it clear that it is a solicitation.

Why would a homeowner, or anyone else for that matter, think they have to respond because the letter *is from a lawyer?*

Because lawyers, doctors, and car mechanics know things. More importantly, they know how things work. Inside knowledge. That instills authority whether it is warranted or not.

When your mechanic tells you that you sheared the transmorgerfer gears in the sprocaxle – and he does it in German, Swedish, and Japanese – you nod along and write a check. When your doctor tells you that after running four miles you need a dose of Dihydrogen Oxide, you nod and write her a check.

The man described above who was told to pack his bags responded to one of my letters.

212

I wish I could stamp "I'M ON YOUR SIDE" or "AN ADVOCATE FOR YOU" in red caps on the letters I send out to potential clients instead of ADVETISING MATERIAL designed to warn and deter. But I respect the rules and the reasons for them so I'm thrilled when someone in need sees past the big red stamp and calls and asks for help.

§

Ignorance is bliss until it isn't.

I keep struggling with why people don't reach out to lawyers when they have a legal problem. I'd like to think the same people who let a legal problem get bad before seeking out help are the same people who wait until a health problem gets bad before going to a doctor.

Or, maybe, people don't really know they have a serious legal problem. It's probably never as obvious as a health problem.

There are those who hold out as long as they can and not seek help who fall into the category of, "I was told this will all work out soon, so I didn't think I needed help."

An example of this is when someone who is late on their mortgage is told, "Just make next month's payment, don't worry about it this month."

This was what a woman who called my office told me. Then she wondered why her credit report showed late payments for 8 months. Because when she missed a month, and just paid the next month, she

213

was really paying the last month's payment, and so she continued to be late each month after that. Should the bank have told her this would happen? Of course it should have. But banks aren't in the business if *NOT* making money, and when you are late, they make money.

The lesson here is she had a problem and took the first person's word for it on how to solve it, and then it got worse.

It's tough to seek legal help (especially because the world assumes lawyers are going to have a high price tag), when you think the solution is right around the corner or you are told "Just do this, just do that" by your bank and you'll be ok. I think I understand and maybe I'd even hesitate to reach out to an attorney and pay a fee too if I thought the problem was going to be solved, at no out of pocket cost to me, in a matter of weeks, days or hours.

How long would you hold out if you continued to feel sick? A parallel example is talking to a nurse friend of yours when you are sick and she gives you some medical advice. That advice doesn't seem to work and you probably then just go to the doctor.

People I talk to whose legal problems are far down the track don't exactly seek advice from a paralegal (the equivalent of a nurse in this example), and then immediately go find an attorney if they don't get better.

Usually people talk to their brother in law who is an insurance guy, then to their boss who is a smart guy, who refers them to an accountant … Each person has an opinion, and because many legal issues are emotionally charged, these advice-givers commiserate with you but you never get closer to having a real answer to your legal problem. Meanwhile the legal problem chugs along down the track.

Then there are the people who are ignorant or in denial, or both. If they know anything about the legal issue they have, they tend to hope it will go away if they don't pay attention to it. When it comes to legal issues surrounding debt, it's interesting how people respond this way, as opposed to how they would probably respond to getting arrested or fighting for custody of their children. Somehow having a legal issue that is caused by debt is some intangible cloud that has settled in but doesn't change what your reality looks like on a day to day basis. You can just go another day without dealing with it. Until you can't anymore.

I was hired by a young man who works for our prison system. A good, steady job. His wife works too. But one thing led to another earlier in the year and they couldn't make the mortgage payment for a few months, then they couldn't afford to catch up. This apparently had happened before but the first time they did catch up. This time he was waiting to be able to save up enough to pay off all the back payments but at the same time the bank was pushing the case forward. When he came to my office he even had a vital form all filled out that would have slowed the case down and shown the bank he wanted to save his house but he just never filed it. One or two days longer before seeking legal help and this guy would have lost his house completely.

I can't figure out if he was waiting for the problem to go away or if he just didn't think there was a problem.

If it's fear or assumption that an attorney is going to be "too expensive," think about these nuggets:

I had to charge this new client more because he came to me at the last minute. We had no time to prepare, I had to drop what I was doing and concentrate on his case alone for a day, write motions, fill out forms, make calls to get his case especially assigned to the next available court date. If the excuse is, "I can't afford an attorney," please try looking for a lawyer sooner than later. It only gets more expensive.

Then think about what is the cost of losing your house and then having to move. Most homeowners in this country are living much cheaper with a mortgage payment than they would be if they rented an apartment.

With each mortgage payment, you generally earn equity in the home, but this is not so when you make a monthly rent payment. In my state, the foreclosure process can take many months, so the longer you hang onto the house, even if you are going to lose it eventually, the more money you can save.

If a lawyer can keep you in your house longer, and the cost of the lawyer is about 1/3 per month of the mortgage payment or what renting an apartment would cost (never mind moving expenses, changing your kids' schools, etc.), then you are coming out ahead even if you do commit to paying legal fees.

§

I initially assume that anyone I talk to who is in foreclosure wants to save the house. Most people do. Some people will say, "Yes, I want to, but you know, I probably can't afford it anymore, but I'd stay if it were affordable." Others know they don't want to keep it but they just need time to figure things out.

The perfectionist in me wants to save all the houses. I assume that if someone wants to save their home they haven't even contemplated alternatives. Sometimes I will get months into the representation and the client will finally say, "It's OK if this doesn't work out, I've been thinking of moving in with my daughter who lives in Florida." Oh, I think, of course. They lost a lot of sleep over this before even hiring me, it makes sense that they have developed a Plan B or an exit plan. It's great that I can buy them the time needed to find a place to go and clean out the house and decide what to bring with them so they don't have to do it in a rush.

Sometimes I just can't save the house. I'll often see this coming from the first meeting with the client. Homeowners tend to feel stuck, like they have to stay in the house when they go into foreclosure. In my state the process can take so long that this can cause homeowners to really stagnate in a property they no longer want but they assume they must stay in to deal with the foreclosure.

I love being able to tell people they have options, such as just walking away. I seem to have this conversation a couple of times per month with people who come into the office for advice. I like to not only tell people they are not married to the house, but I like to give them some ideas on where they can go and what they can do.

I told someone else that I heard the southwest region of France has been found to be a very affordable place to live. Sounds great to me. I often suggest to retired couples that they may find second acts as English teachers in Costa Rica. That also sounds good to me.

I hope and expect to start getting postcards from former clients from these exotic locations any day now.

§

Some houses have so many memories. That can make it very hard for people to accept that they just can't stay anymore. I recently had a potential client who said it perfectly: "I got married in this house. I raised my kids in this house. It's my neighborhood." Hopefully he will be able to keep his house but he may just have to come up with an exit plan. Some people are OK with leaving the memories behind, especially after divorce. It helps if they have the time to find someplace to move to where they don't have to uproot the kids from their schools and they don't have to adjust to a completely new neighborhood or community.

I recently worked with a couple who hung on and hung on to their house for as long as they could. They had raised a son and two daughters in the home and liked the location. Their son had since gone off into the service, and the girls were college age. I of course assumed it would be tragic for this family group to lose this home. I learned halfway in that the house needed a lot of work, one of the daughters spent a lot of time at her boyfriend's apartment and the other daughter was looking for an apartment with her friends. Soon it was going to be just the two parents anyways. Given enough time, they found an apartment for themselves one town over and from the way they described it, it was going to be just the two of them again like it was before they had children. Sounds nice to me.

15. Letting go

In the areas of law I practice in, the bulk of the cases are prosecuted by only a handful of firms and lawyers.

Foreclosure is all these lawyers do and they are very efficient at their jobs. By my estimate, just two Connecticut firms handle about 9,000 foreclosure matters at any given time, all with just a relatively small number of lawyers.

By necessity, those firms operate by the numbers – a homeowner isn't a person, just a number, a file, a target, a quota to fill. Homeowners who try to go it alone, who use the Internet for help, or just plain wing it are shocked to find that their cases don't receive personal attention.

Homeowners are constantly surprised to find that the person on the "other side" doesn't seem to care about helping them. I have to explain, over and over, that in defiance of logic and common sense, the lenders and their attorneys don't treat individual homeowners like individuals. There is no "treatment" at all because computers make the decisions and while sometimes a human interprets the data they are still a slave to the stats. When a homeowner goes it alone, the homeowner pretty much ends up hitting a brick wall more often than not.

I recent years, I've become as quick and efficient at defending foreclosure matters as the banks have in taking houses. I have pretty much seen it all when it comes to homeowner hardship, procedural and computer error and dealing with the humans on the other end of those computers. I, too, spend all day every day honing my foreclosure skills, but not for the banks. I only represent homeowners.

What do you get when you put one lawyer skilled at foreclosing and one lawyer skilled at defending a foreclosure in a court room together? You get a shot at saving your home. You get a shot at having all the information so the process makes sense. You get a voice. You get a fair fight.

§

I get foreclosure clients at various stages of the process. Very rarely these days do I start with someone at the beginning of the case or, best case scenario, someone who knows they are about to go into foreclosure and wants to plan their response.

I take so many clients who are at the end of the line I feel like the patron saint of lost cause foreclosures.

There are a lot of reasons people wait. Some of this book is my effort at understanding why they wait.

The ramifications of this trend hit home with me every time I spend a Monday morning in short-calendar. In one recent session (in just one court out of about 14 throughout the state) there were a little over one hundred items on the docket that day. One hundred decisions that a judge has to make.

This is an example of how my state's courts are jammed with foreclosure cases. It's a sad fact and it's not going to change anytime soon. When overwhelmed by work, it's basic human nature to shortcut the work pile – especially the tedious. That day, besides me, the judge, the clerk, and a marshal, there were eight other people in the room. For one hundred motions. Two attorneys representing the banks (yes, these two had *every* case), me, and a handful of homeowners there to speak up.

There are two sides to every argument, but only if two sides show up. On that day, out of one hundred motions, the judge heard seven arguments. Ninety-three motions were decided by default judgment. But those that did appear and speak up got what they asked for. Even if they were near the end of the line of their case.

Just as my state lottery's slogan reminds us: You can't win if you don't play.

§

One of the types of people I see often in my practice is the person who thinks they are tied to their property. As discussed throughout this book, the average American wants to "do the right thing" and so subscribes to so many myths that they think are "the right thing" to do.

Sticking with a property in foreclosure, even if they don't want to save it, falls into what they believe is the right thing to do. There is teeth gnashing, hand-wringing and lots of "I have to do this" and "I have to do that" going on when someone is in foreclosure, but equal amounts whether the homeowner wants to keep the home or not.

Many people, once they fall behind on their mortgage, realize they were paying too much for a mortgage, especially after a divorce or life-changing crisis. What once was their dream house now just seems like a money pit. Having to write that mortgage check out of an income half or even one-third of what used to come into the household becomes paralyzing.

They sit at my conference room table not even aware of an option they have: they can just walk away.

Sometimes it takes me half the meeting to realize the client would walk away if they knew they could. The initial problem is they tell me they want to keep the property. This is usually just a reaction to believing they must keep the property or thinking this is the right thing to do. They equate staying in the property as "keeping" the property. Alternatively, they believe that being in the foreclosure process binds them to the home, as if suddenly NOT paying your mortgage means you turn into the home's caretaker for the bank.

There really is a personification of the bank by homeowners in foreclosure; they believe one or more of the following: an actual person has made the decision to start the foreclosure; an actual person is watching what they do; an actual person is angry that they have fallen behind on payments; and that they have to please this person, keep up the condition of the property and make sure nothing happens to it.

That's not a bad way to be—I am not saying that falling behind on your mortgage should be the slippery slope down which your sense of right and wrong slides, that you should vandalize or otherwise destroy the property. But when it guides your every decision—whether to stay at a job you hate or for which you are underpaid, whether you visit or care for ailing parents or otherwise put your life on hold—that is when I wish there wasn't so much gobbledygook on the Internet, or spewing from my clients' co-workers' or in-laws' mouths about your rights when you're in foreclosure.

A lot of time and energy is wasted because of these myths.

I have met with so many people over the years who are all in a similar financial predicament that I am good at judging personalities, hobbies, interests, etc.

For example, when a client didn't understand that a home mortgage was a secured loan, and I was trying to explain that the bank could take the home, I took a stab and used the example of borrowing money to purchase a Harley Davidson—and to this client, it all became clear.

I have developed a script of sorts that I use when a client feels stuck in their house because it's in foreclosure and they think they can't

224

sell it or they must stay in it until the foreclosure process has completely run its course. I love having this conversation because someday I too will be at a crossroads with my house and it's so liberating.

I remember the first time I had this conversation, probably because it felt good to read the client correctly. She was in her mid-to-late fifties, either never married or divorced, no children. Graying, short hair, she wore dangly earrings, a blouse that looked like it was made in India and a long flowy skirt. And based on that, the conversation from which I developed the "script" went something like this:

Me: "You know you don't have to stay in the house."

Client: "I don't? I thought that when you're in foreclosure you can't put the house on the market, you have to stay there. My brother-in-law says (fill in the blank with some crap this guy picked up somewhere) … The bank calls all the time, what if I didn't take their calls?"

Me: "You'll be fine. You don't need to talk to the bank. They know you're behind and you can't pay—just like a million other Americans. You can move out, you can list it for sale. You can leave if you want, anytime."

Client: "But I thought I had to stay."

Me: "I know. But you don't."

Client: "I hadn't thought of that before. Are you sure?"

Me: "Yes, and you know what?" I sat back in my chair and looked

225

her up and down, "I see you in Santa Fe."

Client: "What do you mean?"

Me: "You can move. You can go anywhere. And I see you . . . in Santa Fe."

Client: "How can I afford that?"

Me: "I don't know. But the Internet is a magical thing—just go online tonight and look up the cost of an apartment in Santa Fe or Albuquerque, check out what the job market is like there. Just look. You never know."

Client: "Hmmm... you know, my sister lives in Tampa, and she keeps telling me I can stay with her until I get settled down there… and our mother lives down there too…"

And there you go. I read her as the Santa Fe type, but the conversation was the push she needed to realize she could just walk away and be in a warmer climate closer to family.

THAT is the right thing to do.

§

On the flip side of this – the person who can't make a decision, can't quite decide to walk, can't quite commit to staying and just . . . well, tries to get by – there's this:

Wired magazine made a big splash – viral level – when they wrote a feature article about Amazon's CamperForce.

If you've never heard of it, it's the official designation (really) for the army of retired folk in RVs who travel the country for seasonal work at Amazon Fulfillment Centers around the country.

It's an amazing thing. Amazon recruits at campsites around the country. Retired folk get three months or more of more than full-time employment (there's tons of overtime if anyone wants it), Amazon gives out a lot of freebies (including ibruprofen), and Amazon gets a mature work force that is diligent and responsible.

It's a fascinating read about two subcultures - RVers and CamperForce. What jumped out at me, though, was the story within the story, the story of the two main protagonists, Chuck and Barb. Chuck and Barb had a nice condo in Myrtle Beach. They owned a business and were enjoying life before the Recession hit. They lost their retirement funds in 2008 courtesy of Wells Fargo, and the business - adventure tours - tanked with the economy. They tried for four years to pay their credit cards, mortgage, and bills, pouring everything into a vain effort to save their condo and salvage their credit scores.

They lost everything, sold their possessions, Barb's brother sold them a 29-foot 1996 National RV Sea Breeze motor home for $500. It had a dead generator, dry-rotted tires, and a leak in the gas line. They got it up and running, barely, it leaked everywhere in heavy rain. They wandered the country surviving on Chuck's (early) social security payments and odd jobs. Amazon's CamperForce was a godsend.

Somewhere along the line Chuck and Barb ran into a couple of other RVers, also on the road because of the the Recession. Their new friends were fairly new to the road too. They were about to join the CamperForce for the first time, though their needs were nowhere near those of Chuck and Barb. They had a state-of-the-art RV and threw great cookouts.

The two couples were roughly the same ages. They both lost their houses to the Recession. But, here's the difference between them - the thing that struck me so hard - Chuck and Barb's new friends had simply walked away from their house in Oregon. When the value of their home tanked well below the amount they owed, they did the math, assessed their other assets and debts and walked. They didn't waste years and every penny they had to save the house; they knew they didn't have the assets, equity or income to do any more than tread water with no end in sight. So they walked.

It is the perfect example of what I've been preaching for a long time now - you can plan for a foreclosure and use it as an opportunity. No path is written in stone and you can explore all the options. Try seeing yourself in Santa Fe.

16. Last Words

It bears repeating how well *The Big Short* did as good a job as anything in any medium in explaining the housing bubble and ensuing chaos. The story is incredibly frustrating and infuriating. In so entertainingly showing us the how and whys of what happened, the utter lack of a 'happy' ending was shattering but realistic. A few people got rich, millions lost their homes, the guys that perpetuated it all were bailed out and moved on to new investments and new bonuses. Fairness, never mind justice, was not part of the equation.

I was sitting with a few of the still millions of Americans dealing with the continuing ramifications of, according to the movie (very persuasively), an enormous scam. As the credits rolled we were left with Steve Carell's scathing indictment of Wall Street and Ryan Gosling's slick, sarcastic denouement ... and nothing else.

No solutions, no "at least the bad guys were held accountable," no "things changed and this will never happen again...." Nothing.

Still, I think it's important for everyone to know what happened, and how it happened. Then file it away, remember but bury the righteous indignation, anger and frustration because - as *The Big Short* so clearly shows us - it has no impact whatever on anything.

That's not quite true, all that does have an impact in foreclosure defense: it gets in the way. My clients and I are not going to undo anything that came out of the greatest, most devastating financial meltdowns of our lifetimes in a court, regardless of our anger.

All we can - and will - do is use everything available under the law to do everything possible to get the best solution. We'll leave the angst and revenge fantasies to Hollywood.

§

Several years ago, I read an interesting perspective on the phenomenon that is television. TV was described as a stranger that we all allow into our homes even though if all that it brought with it were packaged as a person, we would never let him in the door.

Think about that—we turn on our televisions and we allow countless voices, images, points of view, violence, shock, horror, and all kinds of messages about society and ourselves pour out into our living rooms (and now bedrooms, kitchens and even bathrooms).

I'm not saying television isn't great and hasn't revolutionized our culture. I'm saying that we used to live without it. Many Americans still do, but those of us who turn our TVs on are subject to anything that comes out of "the box" unless we employ a simple tool that does more than change the station: it's the mute button.

Let's say you sit down to watch a half hour of a comedy show. The content of the show only takes up about 22 minutes of every half hour of television, and the remainder is commercial breaks. That's 8 minutes per half hour, and at least 16 minutes per hour of messages about food, video games, toys, credit cards, cars, vacations, personal hygiene products, fantasy sports websites, medications, you name it. And we don't have to listen to any of it. We can hit the mute button.

I probably started employing this trick when I first got a TV with a remote control, sometime in my mid-twenties. I think I started because the commercials were louder than the actual show and they annoyed me. I'd just hit mute and my world became a little more peaceful.

During law school, I probably watched every re-run of *NYPD Blue* and *Law and Order*, all with a textbook on my lap so I could read during the muted commercials. When I first started dating my husband, he thought I was strange for doing this, but he soon saw the benefit—we could spend that much more time talking (or doing other things) during commercial breaks. When we introduced (or tried to introduce) this habit to my husband's family while visiting over holidays, they thought it was strange.

I was hoping they would catch on because his sister has a young son, and I thought it would make *HER* life easier if they muted the ads so that her son would be less likely to be influenced by the messages television sends to children (which I think can be safely boiled down to "spend your parents' money" and "eat this crappy food").

There was resistance; it's true that some ads are so funny or outrageous that if you do not see them, you miss out on a lot of "water cooler" conversation about them at work or school. My father-in-law's reaction was that he was afraid he'd miss part of his show if he couldn't hear the end of the commercial break.

I've been muting ads for so long and so habitually that I'll see the same ad for weeks and not know what is said. Eventually, we'll forget to hit mute and I'll get to listen to the ad and I'll say, "Oh, that's what that commercial is about? I have seen it a million times but I have never heard it!" But once really is enough.

One interesting thing I noticed about commercials is that after the economic crash in 2008 and 2009, there was a huge reduction in ads for credit cards.

Prior to the crash, ads for all the big credit card vendors - Discover, Chase, Capital One, Bank of America - flooded the airwaves. The one card that seemed to survive the crash was Capital One. That company continued to push consumer credit cards consistently when others had completely left the market, or had at least stopped spending on advertising.

While I was happy to see fewer ads for credit cards, it's interesting to note that Capital One seemed to be the lone survivor. How Capital One was able to do this is a discussion for another day.

Since the point of advertising is to sell to us, the message is that we should spend our money. I've never taken a marketing class, but repetition seems to be a key factor in the effectiveness of advertising.

The first time you see an ad for McDonald's French fries, it may not even register. But the tenth or eleventh time, especially if you're now seeing the ad while hungry, can be very powerful.

Same with ads for new cars. For the most part, if our cars can accommodate our family sizes and other basic transportation needs, we could all drive our cars until they fall apart. But we are bombarded with ads for new cars that include enticements such as credit for brand loyalty and low interest rate loans, so the next time we go out to the driveway we are more likely to see our cars as sub-par and start considering upgrading (that is, spending money we didn't intend to spend prior to being bombarded by the ad campaign, and spending money we probably shouldn't spend or don't even have).

If you're working on improving your diet or your finances (or both), muting out these messages that are designed purely to get us to buy can really help.

Give it a try. Ready, aim, mute.

§

A friend of mine tells this story from his law school days – just another reminder that your financial condition today neither defines you or your future.

December 1991, I came out of New York Law School at 11:30 pm after a five-hour Constitutional Law final. Cold, windy, raw, the World Trade Tower looming a few blocks away- I thought it ugly then, miss it now – I did not have it in me to hike over to City Hall and the Lexington

233

Avenue Express to Grand Central. Alone on the corner of Church and Worth, I flagged down a cab, jumped in, skipped eye contact with the driver, an average looking guy who gave me a surprising, pleasant "Hello, where to?"

I responded with a mumbled, "Grand Central, don't take Park," nestled into the corner, eschewed the seatbelt, pulled my bag tight to my side, closed one eye, kept the other half opened to insure he did indeed stay away from Park. Took a bump on Sixth that forced me to open both eyes, I scanned the glass divider, taped to it behind the driver was a picture of Grant.

I looked at it, stared at it, held my curiosity for half a block before asking, "Why do you have a picture of Ulysses S Grant on the glass?"

"Ah, you know him." He sounded surprised – which, if you dwell on it, is perhaps a bit disturbing.

"Of course," I answered, but not in that tone reserved for cab drivers who insist on engaging in conversation at exactly the moment you are in no mood to talk to anyone, never mind the stranger driving you the long way to your destination. "So why his picture?"

"I just turned forty," he announced, and I knew at once where this was going and sat up. "And I'm driving a cab, trying to finish school, kinda' the loser's track, you know? So, I put that photo there to remind me that when

234

Grant was forty he was bankrupt, lived with his wife and kids in his father's house, worked as a clerk in a feed store . . . talk about losers. . . eight years later he was President of the United States . . . that's it, man, nothing's ever over."

Yeah, that's it. One day you're in foreclosure or filing for bankruptcy, the next you're president. Nothing is ever really over.

Acknowledgements

I don't deal with files, I deal with people. Lots of people that other lawyers don't help because they don't think they can afford legal help. I would like to thank all the clients who have trusted their circumstances to me and who have made the investment in their problem to hire me and my team to help them.

My exposure to the legal world started long before law school, when I was hired as a reader and driver for a blind attorney, Kathryn Mobley. Working with her made me see that lawyers can make a difference in the world, and she inspired me to give it a try. Without Dan Blinn who hired me right out of law school to work on consumer protection cases, who knows where I'd be today. Donna Convicer, a veteran foreclosure defense attorney, kept me centered and guided my advocacy as my law practice grew. My parents taught me everything I know about money- the value of a dollar, when to spend and when to bargain. This book would never have come together without Roland Hicks, writer and editor and cultural and political vanguard for my writing.

Last but not least, my husband Paul continues to be the

voice of reason and keeps me moving in the right direction.

About the Author

Sarah Poriss owns and operates the largest foreclosure defense firm in Connecticut and has worked exclusively in the area of consumer protection since finishing law school in 2002.

Her blog was named to the ABA's Top 100 law related blogs nationwide in 2015 and 2016.

Sarah is an active member of the Connecticut Bar and has – and will continue to – testify in Legislative hearings on any measures that may affect her clients.

Sarah has appeared on NPR and makes frequent appearances on Connecticut TV stations to discuss debt and credit matters.

Sarah traded in her speed skates (yes, you read that correctly) for running shoes in 2015 when she decided to run a half-marathon. Shortly after completing the race, she grabbed a bike and added triathlons to her schedule, and is now hitting trails building up to off-road marathons.

For more about Sarah please check out her website at

www.sarahporiss.com

Index

·

Made in the USA
Middletown, DE
05 June 2020